The Coaching Leader

Typeset by BookPOD

ISBN: 978-0-6456220-0-3 (paperback) 978-0-6456220-1-0 (ebook)

A catalogue record for this book is available from the National Library of Australia

THE COACHING LEADER

Essential Skills to Enhance
Your Leadership and Develop
Your People Every Day

Clifford Morgan

Acknowledgements

It was Sir Isaac Newton who famously said, 'If I have seen further, it is by standing on the shoulders of giants.' This is how I feel about this book. I would not be in the position I am today, nor would this book have been written, if it were not for the many people who have contributed to my journey and my growth over the years. While many of these individuals may not have a global reputation one would associate with a giant within their industry, they are giants in my world, absolutely making world-class contributions to me as a leader. While my gratitude extends to many, I have named just a few below without whom these pages would not have been filled.

Firstly, the truly exceptional Jane Anderson. As a business coach she has transitioned me from consultant to thought leader, taking my business and I to a whole new level. While writing a book had been in the back of my mind for many years, it was Jane who shook, poked and prodded me into putting pen to paper. It is only with her continued guidance, encouragement and accountability I have been able to finish this project.

If you read sections of this book and think, 'That was well written,' you can thank Kristen Lowrey. Editor extraordinaire, Kristen took the ramblings of this old Air Force 'grunt' and turned them into something coherent.

I cannot mark any milestone in my career as a psychologist, coach and leader without acknowledging the profound impact of Dr Mike

Allan. As a supervisor he served as an important role model, being the first organisational psychologist I knew who did the work I wanted to do - coaching senior executives. Over the years his friendship has continued to challenge me, stretching my identity and thinking, shaping who I am today.

It would not be an exaggeration to say the art and practice of coaching has changed my life. I am therefore eternally grateful to Natalie Ashdown from Open Door Coaching Group for introducing me to the world of coaching. As part of the Air Force Leadership Coaching Program, it was under Natalie's tutelage that I first learned the skill set that has shaped not only my career but also the rest of my life. While my coaching practice has evolved over time, I can trace much of my thinking back to what Natalie first taught me at the picturesque RAAF Glenbrook all those years ago. If anyone is looking for formal coaching accreditation, I have no hesitation in recommending Open Door Coaching Group.

Finally, the most important acknowledgement goes to my wife and business partner, Mara Morgan. Not only does she keep our business moving forward, she manages to hold our family together as well. She has worn the frustrations and shared the joys as she travelled beside me on the roller coaster of a journey writing this book has been. Without her, this book would not have been written. I truly could not do what I do today without her constant, steadying support.

Contents

Introduction

There is an activity I use to start many of my workshops. It was first introduced to me by my good friend, coach and master facilitator, Darryl Stubberfield. And it involves potatoes and straws.

Potatoes and straws

In this activity everyone in the group is provided with one large potato and as many plastic straws as they would like. The brief from there is simple – put the straw through the middle of the potato. No other objects can be used. Only the straws and the potatoes.

When I explained the parameters of the activity, I would often receive looks of incredulity and comments from half the room about it being impossible, while the other half fired off a barrage of questions trying to find a loophole they could exploit. Eventually each person would resign themselves to the task and turn their attention to how they might achieve it.

I want you to stop and consider your approach if you were in the room. What would you try?

Over the years I saw many inventive strategies employed. I've seen straws bent into a myriad of different shapes to try and improve their cutting / digging ability. I've seen multiple straws squeezed into another straw in an attempt to strengthen the host straw. I saw some repeatedly bang potatoes on top of straws, and straws onto potatoes.

I've seen people try to suck bits of potato out using the straw. And in every group there is always someone who takes two straws and sticks one on each side of the potato and tries to convince me that it is in fact a single straw going right through.

Eventually the majority of the room would resort to trying to gently push their straw into the potato while rotating it, as if to screw the straw into the potato. They would then pull a small chunk of potato out, remove it and repeat the process. It was a tedious, time consuming process but each time they pulled their straw out they made a small amount of progress. Eventually they would complete the task.

Once the task was completed, the room would be in a complete mess. Small chunks of potato and a multitude of mangled and destroyed straws would litter desks and table tops. As I began to debrief the activity, I would ask about the different tactics people used and we would laugh at some of the more humorous attempts in the group. But eventually we would hone in on what actually worked – the screwing tactic.

Most people are able to explain that past experience has taught them that if they want to use one object to create a hole in another, screwing is generally effective. While this approach did allow most people to achieve the objective of the task, it was minimally effective at best. It was not terribly efficient (it was tedious work), it was resource intensive (there were a lot of straws used) and it was destructive (both potatoes and straws were destroyed in the process).

But once the participants tried this strategy and found a little bit of success, most reported having the thought, 'If I keep doing this, I'll eventually get there'. So they 'locked on' to this particular tactic and doubled down their efforts to complete the task. Once they had locked on to this approach, they stopped looking for other potential solutions, unconsciously shutting out any other options and approaches to the task. Interestingly few people were ever aware that they had become so focused they had stopped looking for a better way to achieve their goal.

Potatoes and straws in leadership

Just as the participants in the workshops would get 'locked in' on the first solution that brought even a bit of success, leaders in the workplace can fall victim to the same rigid thinking. In fact, I frequently encounter leaders who rely heavily on their past experiences (usually from early in their careers) to inform how they handle situations in the work environment. And, generally, this approach doesn't lead to the best results.

It may be the way they complete a task, deal with conflict, influence people or conduct performance reviews. But when they're trapped in that rigid way of thinking, they rarely stop to consider what might be the best approach for this specific situation within this specific context. Instead, they jump right in, relying on what they've always done. Even though that approach might only be minimally effective, they latch on to the small amount of progress they've made in the past, adopting the 'I'll get there eventually' thought process.

These leaders may or may not eventually achieve the desired outcome, but they almost always leave carnage in their wake – wasted resources, broken people and messy situations. The kicker is that these messy results could have been avoided if only they had taken some time to look at the available options before acting. They could have come up with an approach that was efficient, effective and empathic – and tailored for the situation at hand. And they could have achieved better results than expected and built people up in the process.

Instead, they 'locked on' to a single way of responding, and 'locked out' the possibility of identifying any better approaches. All while being completely unaware that any decision making was taking place.

Learning to 'unlock' your leadership skills

This concept of 'locking on and locking out' is useful in helping people begin to understand what coaching is and how it can help hone essential leadership skills. Everyone has the ability and resources to find effective solutions to their own problems. And leaders have the ability to find effective solutions to problems in the workplace. Sometimes they just need a little bit of help to realise it.

Coaching, as a process, helps people to 'unlock', take a step back and view things from a different perspective. In so doing, people see things – new information, extra resources, other options – that they weren't able to before. From this new perspective they can identify different, more effective, approaches than those they may have tried in the past.

It had always been within their capabilities to choose and implement these approaches. They just had to 'unlock' first. And it was through the process of coaching that they were able to do just that.

In this book

This book will equip you with the leadership skills you need to help you and your team 'unlock' from old approaches, identify new and more effective ones and unleash levels of performance and potential yet to be discovered. As an organisational psychologist and executive coach I've worked with many leaders and teams over the years, applying these skills and seeing amazing results. I've also spent the last decade teaching these skills to leaders who use them to coach their teams while they lead.

The results achieved by leaders who intentionally embrace, develop and employ these skills within their teams, are often astounding – far exceeding both my expectations and theirs.

I hope you enjoy this book. I hope you find it valuable and are inspired to take what is written in these pages and apply it in your workplace. In doing so you'll become a better leader of more capable and high-performing people and teams.

~ Clifford Morgan

Note: For those still wondering about the potatoes, there was a trick – or more accurately, a more effective approach. If you place your thumb over the end of the straw, you create an airlock, trapping the air inside the straw and thereby strengthening it. With a little bit of practice, coordination and accurately applied force, you can punch the straw straight through the middle of the potato, achieving the task in a single second using only one straw and creating no mess.

While the reduction of single use plastics has great benefit for the environment, it has meant the disappearance of plastic straws. You can try this using paper straws, however the results are less reliable and all too often the straw crumbles. Alas, I now resort to different activities to open my workshops.

CHAPTER ONE

Leadership today

'Leaders don't create followers,
they create more leaders.'
– Tom Peters

When I was growing up, I wanted to be a fighter pilot. My grandfather, after whom I'm named, was a pilot. He flew C-47 Dakotas in World War II. Known as one of the 'Biscuit Bombers', he would fly over the Kokoda Trail in Papua New Guinea, dropping food, ammunition and other supplies by parachute to the Australian troops fighting the Japanese below.

While I never got to meet my grandfather (he died before I was born), I grew up wanting to be like him. I wasn't the only one in the family – I also have two uncles, three cousins and a brother who are all pilots. And I've had a career in the Air Force that has spanned 16 years. You might say flying and the aviation industry is in my blood.

At the time of writing, my brother is a First Officer (FO) for QANTAS, Australia's premier airline. Having flown internationally for several years, he now flies domestic routes across Australia. As an FO, it's his role to act as co-pilot for the captain of the aircraft. The co-pilot is there to assist and support the captain.

My brother describes the difference between a good captain and a poor one, and it doesn't necessarily come down to skills. In fact, a technically excellent pilot may be a very poor captain, particularly if they don't communicate well or facilitate the FO's ability to support the flying of the aircraft. Poor captains do all the flying themselves, make all the decisions themselves and do all the thinking and planning themselves.

On the one hand, this approach is understandable. After all, the captain is ultimately responsible for the safety of the aircraft and all its passengers. However, flying with this sort of captain is usually not enjoyable and often boring for the FO. Worse, they fail to learn or grow in their role. Instead, they disengage, sit there and drink coffee the entire flight.

Flying with a good captain, however, is a different story altogether. Good captains invite the FO to contribute during the flight planning and discuss their decisions while on the ground and in the air. They encourage the FO to ask questions, check calculations and challenge thinking. And they allow the FO to do the majority of the flying, remaining ready to step in if the FO encounters any challenges.

While the captain retains the overall responsibility and accountability for the flight of the aircraft, in many ways a good captain will support the FO flying the aircraft, rather than the other way around. They are there to correct, guide and advise, and to take control if something goes wrong. But they are intentional about allowing the FO to get the experience they need to become a future captain.

A good captain prepares an FO for their future. And a good leader in the workplace does the same.

The responsibility of leaders – primary vs secondary level

As a leader, you have a primary or surface-level responsibility to help your people to perform and achieve common goals. What those goals are and what constitutes good performance will vary depending on the company, organisation or context you are in. What doesn't change is the secondary or deeper-level responsibility. That is the responsibility to develop the *experience* and *expertise* of your people.

In corporate and business settings, plenty of focus is typically given to this surface-level responsibility. We set the organisational strategy, articulate key objectives and targets. We develop clear KPIs and goals for our teams and monitor performance to keep them focused on producing results. This is logical and desirable, because it's this type of team performance that will ultimately make the company successful, profitable and impactful.

At the same time, only focusing on this surface-level responsibility and the results the team produces is short sighted. The team remains reliant on the leader to provide the results-related leadership tasks (such as taking the organisational strategy and translating it to goals, targets and management) in order to perform. As soon as the leader is removed, or focuses their attention elsewhere, the team begins to struggle and performance dips.

The leader's secondary responsibility of developing people and preparing them to lead is what sustains performance over time. A team filled with highly capable individuals who are also able to lead, will outperform a team of highly-skilled technical experts without leadership capabilities.

When a team has multiple individuals who have cultivated leadership skills and abilities, it has the depth of skills to allow many different individuals to step up when the formal leader of the team moves on. Another team member will be able to seamlessly step into the role and pick up where the previous leader left off. This not only saves the company the costs of recruitment and on-boarding, but also the lost opportunity costs associated with leadership change.

An organisation that is filled with layers of leaders is able to sustain increasing growth and performance.

The workplace today

Today's workplace is different from that of our parents, and it's different from the workplace of ten, five and even three years ago. The pandemic has brought changes to all jobs, regardless of the industry. Of course, there's the increased move to hybrid working arrangements. But there's also been changes in mindset – for example, from thinking about work in terms of 'jobs' and focusing instead on 'capabilities'.

And the changing perspectives and expectations of the workforce globally – particularly with the changing generational demographics of the workforce – have created profound changes in the requirements for work environments.

Jim Rohn, American businessman, author, motivational speaker and Tony Robbins' mentor said, 'The challenge is to become all that you have the possibility of becoming. You cannot believe what it does to the human spirit to maximise your potential and stretch yourself to the limit'.[1] And this is something that today's workforce increasingly embraces.

Today's workplaces are facing the unique challenge of managing the workplace expectations of five different generations. But as millennials are becoming the vast majority of workers, with Gen Z right on their heels, embracing their expectations is the key to success.

When it comes to this generation, workers are not simply driven by monetary reward or even stability. Instead they are looking for development as their primary benefit. Research shows this is even more important than work / life balance, flexibility or bonuses.[2] They want to be able to move up the ladder at work faster and this capability is one of the main attributes of attractive employers today. 'Millennials value workplaces that are collaborative, achievement-oriented, highly creative, positive, diverse, fun, flexible and that provide continuous feedback'.[3]

In order to move up the ladder, workers today are looking for continuous feedback that leads directly into continuous development. And they aren't just looking for a small bump up in one-on-one conversations. In fact, they're looking for up to 50% more.[4]

Despite some anecdotal media reporting, millennials aren't striving to climb the workplace ladder because they are entitled or greedy. It's simply a product of the world they live in. In this time and place everything happens more quickly than ever – including careers. For a millennial worker, progression is the point of the career. And if they don't find this happening for them, the career *feels* meaningless.

These changing perspectives create changing pressures on today's leaders. We need to be able to help our employees find and articulate their meaning and purpose within the workplace, and then find ways to instil that purpose into their working lives.

To do this, we have to start looking at learning agility as one of the most important qualities of employees and recognise the importance of investing in both upskilling and reskilling continuously. We need to be putting time and resources into making these efforts a central part of our workforce management. And we need to be doing all this *now*.

The key challenges for leaders

Unfortunately, leaders today simply aren't equipped for the challenges of the modern workforce. This has nothing (or very little) to do with ability, and much more to do with learning and understanding.

Consider our pilot example – when we toss leaders into the modern workplace, with learnings based on outdated workplace principles and expectations, it's as if we've handed the pilot the controls of an aircraft without ever teaching them how to fly (or better yet, having taught them to fly helicopters but expecting them to fly fighter jets).

It's simply not going to work well.

So, what are the key challenges leaders face in the modern workplace:

- **Lack of training:** Many leaders today – you and others at your organisation included – simply haven't been provided with adequate and forward thinking training.

- **Lack of experience:** Many leaders are also not gaining enough on-the-job experience as they move through the ranks too quickly, or are hired in a managerial role as specialists in a field.

- **Lack of skill development:** Historical leadership training has too often been based around skill acquisition of the leader, and not at all on equipping the leader to develop the skills of those they lead.

When it comes to developing leaders and managers, including teaching them how to develop and empower their own staff, we're falling woefully short. In fact, research shows that the average supervisor will have worked for 10 years before receiving any sort of training.[5] And a full 45% of senior leaders – nearly half – aren't confident in developing their people.[6]

The internal struggle

As I'm working with leaders to navigate these challenges, there are five key frustrations I encounter which they communicate in the following ways:

1. **'We need to find and keep good talent.'**

   The market is more competitive than ever. It's never been easier for staff to leave and find another job. Leaders feel pressured to meet the development needs of their people or risk losing them to competitors who will.

2. **'I wish our teams would be more proactive.'**

   Whether because of a lack of role models, high workloads or company culture, most staff are constantly reactive. They fail to take the initiative and are always on the back foot.

3. **'Our team keeps expecting us to solve problems.'**

   Leaders become the bottleneck, slowing progress and preventing agility when they are relied upon to make decisions and solve problems.

4. **'We are growing beyond the skills of our managers.'**

   Middle leaders often struggle to know how to perform when their role expands. As a company grows, its leaders need to grow with it. Companies who outgrow the skills and capabilities of their people risk collapse.

5. **'We have to do more with less.'**

HR and development needs are becoming more complex, but training budgets aren't increasing. More and more workplace leaders need to bridge the development gap rather than relying on other organisational functions to do so.

As you can see, modern leadership challenges often leave leaders frustrated, filled with doubt and battling mindsets consumed by the threats and risks they face. They struggle against thoughts such as:

'I can't provide the support they need'

Leaders feel the pressure from above and below to do what they haven't been trained for. The organisation wants them to develop capability and staff want to grow. The fear is that if the leader can't support their people to grow, either they'll leave or the organisation will find another leader.

'If this person can't develop, the whole company suffers.'

Challenges with one individual or team are usually far reaching through an organisation. Other teams' performance is hampered every time they have to interact with those individuals, endangering key growth targets and measures of success for the whole company.

'Will we even survive?'

In the face of the increasingly dynamic and competitive market, failure to develop people and the collective capability they provide means the organisation will limp forward rather than thrive. This can leave senior leaders wondering, 'Is it worth it?' or, 'Will we survive at all?'

In an already challenging environment, leaders wrestling with these internal struggles are left experiencing more stress, feeling inadequate and suffering from imposter syndrome. Such a state doesn't promote the performance of the leader or their team. A shift is required to unlock the potential of both leaders and their teams.

The shift

In order for businesses to thrive in the modern world, they need to be filled with high performing, independently thinking and proactive individuals. Leaders need to be developing these characteristics in their staff as well as equipping them to develop these same characteristics in others. This requires a shift to take place. A shift in thinking, a shift in approach, a shift in leadership.

From 'tell' to 'ask'

Most of us know the old proverb – when you give a man a fish, you feed him for the day, but when you teach a man to fish, you feed him for a lifetime. There has never been a time that this is more important in the workplace than today. In fact, it's a vital element for a business to survive in today's disruptive world.

But empowering your employees with the workplace equivalent of fishing lessons is not as easy as simply implementing training or development schemes. Often there are deeply-ingrained hurdles to overcome. After all, most of us have been taught, whether consciously or unconsciously, that being a leader or being in charge is all about telling people what to do. We've been taught that it's the role of the leader to decide what we are doing, where we are going and how and who does what.

You can often see this when children play. They might say, 'I'm the queen (or king)! And you have to do what I say!' The problem is that children are not yet sophisticated enough to understand the benefits of collaboration, or of having layers of leaders. They're still all about the ego, and so they strive to hang onto power.

But if we try to take that tactic as leaders, we'll be about as successful as a child in our roles. That kind of traditional, outdated approach keeps us limited. We are limited, our people are limited and our teams and organisations are limited.

When everything is reliant on the leader, when people are constantly told exactly what to do, they are not empowered. They aren't able to think for themselves. They aren't able to stretch, develop or grow their capabilities. And that is why good leaders stop 'telling' and start 'asking'.

The 'ask' approach is a 'bottom-up, inquisitive, consensus-style approach' while the 'tell' approach is a 'top-down, decisive, command-style approach'.[7] While both styles have their places, asking questions encourages your team to think, engage their brains and become active in the problem-solving process. The more they do this, the more confident they become and the more likely they are to do it again.

Chad Hall, author of *The Coaching Mindset: 8 Ways to Think Like a Coach*, says, 'If the coach thinks the client needs the coach's help and 'heroically' swoops in to save the day, the coach will prevent the client from growing, changing, and saving his own day.'[8]

As leaders we might find ourselves swooping in to save the day more often than we should. When I ask leaders why they do it, most say because it's quicker and easier, and because when something is important we want to ensure that 'it's done right'.

But instead of swooping in, we need to refocus our approach to teaching our team to fish. In other words, teaching them how to save themselves.

This is where coaching comes in.

Reflection time

1. What are the main challenges you face as a leader today?

2. How intentional are you about developing your team? Or is people development an afterthought?

3. When your team brings you a problem, is your first instinct to tell them what to do or ask them a question?

CHAPTER TWO

What is coaching?

'Coaching is unlocking a person's potential to maximise his or her own performance. It is helping them to learn, rather than teaching them.'
– Sir John Whitmore

When I'm running coaching skills training for leaders, I will ask the group a couple of initial questions. These are: what they think coaching is, and what they think coaching is not.

When I ask these questions I usually get a similar set of answers for what coaching is *not*. These generally include phrases like dictating, directing, telling people what to do, belittling, punishing or solving people's problems for them. And they are right. These motivations and actions are definitely *not* coaching.

But while people can typically identify what coaching is *not*, they have a harder time understanding what coaching *is*. When they're able to provide a list of phrases it usually includes words and actions like encouraging, supporting, teaching, equipping, empowering, advising, providing guidance and mentoring. And while many of these things are great activities for leaders to engage in, they don't actually paint a very accurate picture of what coaching is.

More than sports

If I was to walk down the street and stop someone and say the word coaching, what do you think would be the first thing to pop into their head? For the vast majority of people, that thing is going to be the word 'sport'.

Sport is probably the most common activity associated with coaching. Nearly all Australians have had experience with 'coaches' in sport – whether that's Friday arvo sport in primary school, or through extracurricular activities for themselves or their kids. And many of the leaders that I work with and train also have, at some point, coached junior sport.

Coaching in the sporting sphere has one primary aim – skill acquisition. The traditional approach to coaching sport involves introducing a new technique, demonstrating it, teaching it and having players execute or practice it. The coach then watches the team practice and corrects any faults.

Like most people, I have had my fair share of experience being coached in sport. In my first season of playing under sixes soccer as a boy, Mr Pollock, the dad of a schoolmate, was our coach. I have a vivid memory of him coaching us to kick a ball by demonstrating how to use the inside of the foot rather than our toes.

We were lined up behind a ball and had to kick the ball into the goal. As we each took a turn, he would yell, 'Don't kick with your toes!' I'm sure many of you can relate in some way to this experience and in its own way it worked. I certainly will always remember how to kick a soccer ball correctly. It's a skill that I was able to acquire – and at least partly due to coaching.

But when it comes to executive coaching, standing in a room and yelling at your coachees isn't an approach that will get you very far. And a coaching leader needs to see beyond just skills acquisition.

The story of executive coaching

As you might expect, the story of executive coaching in the workplace has its origins in the sporting world, with Sir John Whitmore.

Sir John Whitmore is known as the godfather of modern coaching.[1] He started his own career as a racing car driver in the 1960s. He won both the British and the European Saloon Car Championships and was known as 'the racing baronet' after inheriting the baronetcy of Orsett Estate on the death of his father.

When he retired from elite motorsport, Whitmore embarked on a career coaching tennis, another of his loves. As Whitmore worked with his athletes, he applied the traditional coaching approach, focused on skills improvement. He would show them how to improve their game. He would watch them play and practice the skills he'd shown them. And then he would correct them based on his expertise.

Whitmore found that this tried and true method worked well for a number of his players. But over time he also found that there were quite a few that plateaued. Regardless of what he did to correct their skills, they just wouldn't or couldn't get any better.

Partly out of frustration and partly spurred on by Timothy Gallwey, author of *The Inner Game of Tennis*,[2] John began to ask his players what they thought they needed to do in order to improve their tennis game. Some players thought they needed to change their grip on the racquet. Other players felt they had to change their ball toss when they served. As these players began to identify *for themselves* what they needed to improve or change, their overall tennis game began to improve dramatically.

Whitmore realised that this technique of asking questions and getting athletes to identify what and how they needed to improve seemed to work well. Really well. Soon other coaches began to take note, and the approach began to spread amongst the sporting world. It wasn't long before ski instructors from Scandinavia and golf coaches from Scotland were coming to Whitmore and his team to learn how they might apply this approach to their own students.

A couple of the tennis players that Whitmore was coaching during this time were also senior corporate executives. They encouraged him to see if the same (or substantially similar) techniques might be successful in the corporate world to improve the performance of leaders. Whitmore believed they would.

So, in the 1980s Whitmore and a number of associates started Performance Consulting. With the birth of Performance Consulting came the birth of executive and workplace coaching. They were highly successful. And since then coaching has become one of the most widely recognised forms of leadership development in the workplace.

Defining coaching

Many definitions of coaching exist today. However, I believe that the central essence of each one is captured in the following definition:

> *Coaching is a process of asking strategic questions that enable a person to identify their own solutions to the problems they face and articulate what they need to do to achieve their goals.*

As that definition shows us, coaching is a process.

It isn't magic.

It isn't luck.

It isn't intangible at all.

It is a clearly defined process that is replicable and repeatable in almost any circumstance or industry. While the context may change, and the specific tools and frameworks used may differ, the underlying approach and process remains the same.

Once leaders understand the process, they are able to adopt it and tailor it to almost any situation. If there is an opportunity to learn or to improve (which is pretty much any situation!) then the coaching process applies.

The coaching process

Coaching is a process centred around asking questions. As we articulated in the last chapter, telling people what to do allows them to remain passive and reliant. On the other hand, when we ask questions, we invite them to become actively engaged, both in the situation and in their own development.

Successful coaching isn't just asking any old question. It's about asking strategic questions. These are questions that are intentionally selected to take the coachee on a journey, to help them do the thinking required to grow and improve on the way to achieving desired outcomes.

Strategic questioning encourages the coachee to be engaged and do the hard thinking. It enables people to identify their own ideas and solutions and to generate their own action plans. This process also increases the coachee's level of ownership for the process. By taking them along this journey, the coachee earns the process for themselves, ultimately enabling them to take both themselves and others through the process in the future.

At its core, coaching is about change. It helps people identify what changes they might need to make and how to make them in order to achieve desired outcomes. As Ian Berry writes, 'Coaching is a unique process of human development, one that works to change a person's life for the better and help him/her achieve a number of specific objectives'[3].

The triune focus of coaching – three specific qualities

All leadership is about change. At its most basic level, leadership is about influencing people to make the changes necessary to move closer to a common goal. Of course, there are many techniques and methods that leaders can use to influence people to help them make those required changes. And coaching is one of those techniques.

The best thing about coaching for leaders is that it brings mutual benefits – benefits to the leader and to the employee. That's because it not only empowers people to make changes, but also helps them learn along the way.

For those leaders looking to coach their people, it doesn't have to be complicated. It's simply asking questions that foster three specific qualities.

Triune focus of coaching model

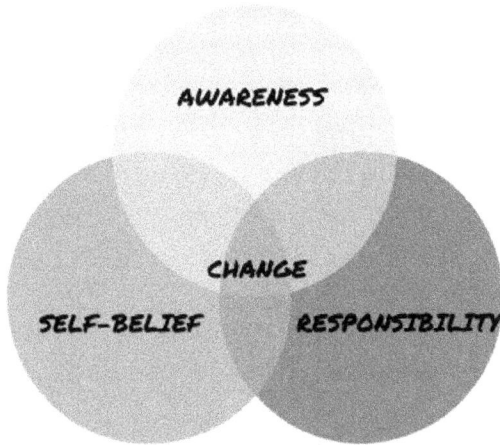

Outlined by the godfather of modern coaching, Sir John Whitmore in his seminal coaching text *Coaching for Performance*, these three qualities are:

1. Awareness
2. Responsibility
3. Self-belief[4]

I call these the triune (which essentially means three in one) focus of coaching because without any one of them, change won't occur.

Awareness

I will often tell people that we are controlled by what we aren't aware of. When we are in a passive state, we aren't in control. Things are being done to us and we are simply reacting to them and the world around us. It's only once we become aware of something, that we have the opportunity to exert any control over it.

When we do become aware, we become engaged. And when we are engaged, we can begin to take control, respond proactively and exert our influence to make change in the world around us.

Of course, even when we become engaged and aware, we simply won't be able to control everything that impacts our lives or our business. We can't control a volatile market, for example, or labour shortages.

We can and should take the opportunity to exert control over the things we can. But in order to do that, we need to be aware of what is inside our control and what is not. We need to understand the real problems we face. And we need to be aware of all the different options and potential solutions.

We also need to be aware that we have the ability to find that solution ourselves and make the changes necessary. And this is part of what good coaching accomplishes. Building awareness so that individuals can take control and pursue change is key to successful coaching.

Responsibility

The next key element to successful coaching is increasing the level of responsibility individuals take for their circumstances and the outcomes they desire. While awareness is required to identify what is inside one's control, it is the sense of responsibility and ownership that is required in order to take action. In fact, it's vital, because it's only a sense of personal responsibility that produces the impetus to change.

Self-belief

In order to take any action, we first need to believe that we can achieve the desired results. In other words, that change is possible. And second we need to believe that we are able to effect that change.

So the role of the coach is to help coachees identify what change is required and then help them to make that change. But it is also their role to help foster the belief that the coachee has the ability to make that change. In psychology this is called self-efficacy.

Self-efficacy is the belief that an individual holds about their ability to influence the world around them.[5] The degree to which individuals believe they can influence their own circumstances and make the changes necessary to achieve the outcomes they desire will determine how likely and motivated they are to make those changes.

Self-belief, along with awareness and responsibility are all necessary for successful change to occur. Each of them facilitate a necessary component of change. Without any one of them, change just won't happen.

So what happens when there is no awareness, no responsibility or no self-belief?

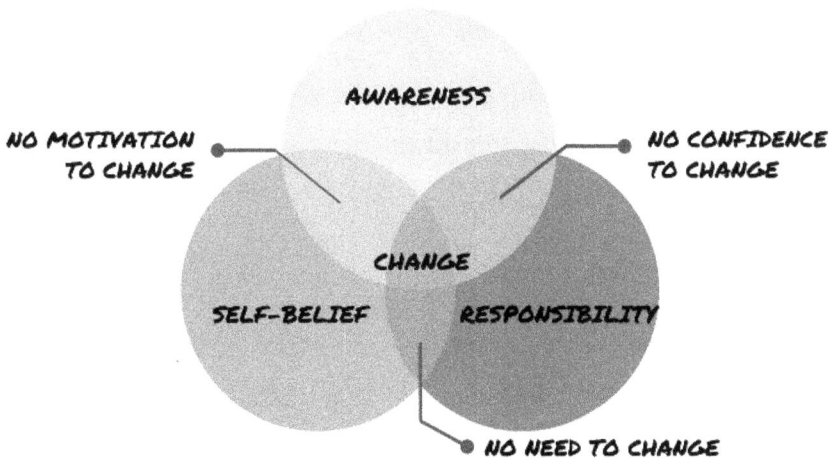

No awareness

Where there is no awareness, there is no need to make a change. People may possess the self-belief and confidence in their ability to make changes, and be willing to take responsibility and own the process. But they have no idea that a change is even needed, let alone what they could do to create that change.

No responsibility

Even if you have the awareness of the need to change and understand what you need to do to make that change, if you don't take responsibility or ownership, there is no impetus or drivers to actually make any changes. The motivation isn't there to overcome the inertia of the status quo.

No self-belief

Change is also not possible where there is no self-belief. Because where there is no self-belief there is no confidence that change is possible. People may be aware of the need for change. They may understand what they need to do to make the change. And they may even recognise that they are responsible for making those changes. However, if they don't believe in their own ability to influence the situation, they won't even attempt to make a change.

The reality is that all three of these qualities are required for people to make changes, whether the desired change is at the individual level, the team level or the organisational level. As leaders, it is our role to foster these three qualities in our people in order to inspire the action required to achieve our collective goals.

Coaching is simply using questions to do so.

Directing vs coaching

As we move into more of a coaching relationship with our teams, we'll find that we're doing less 'directing' and more discussing and advising. This is a natural progression and it's a vital part of coaching. Why? Because the more we direct our staff – the more we tell them what to do and when to do it – the less empowered they are. And the less empowered they are, the less they are able to take responsibility and grow in their role.

Directing vs coaching model

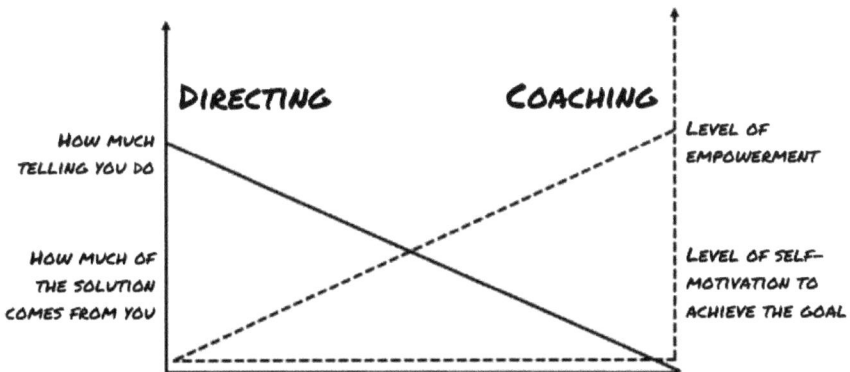

DIRECTING   COACHING

HOW MUCH
TELLING YOU DO

LEVEL OF
EMPOWERMENT

HOW MUCH OF
THE SOLUTION
COMES FROM YOU

LEVEL OF SELF-
MOTIVATION TO
ACHIEVE THE GOAL

While direction may be necessary when skill levels are low and staff are still learning, once they begin to gain competence in their roles, you should steer clear of over directing. Continuing to direct your team past this point can severely curtail their own development and their motivation.

Instead, once someone can complete a task, the next step in their development in that area is to understand how that task fits into the bigger picture. And this needs to be done most efficiently under their own steam. They must learn to understand the why behind that task. They need to fully embrace when it should be conducted, how it should be conducted and, most importantly, how it contributes. But when we continually direct our people, telling them what, when and how to do it, they are less likely to think about and understand the bigger picture. And that means that they are less likely to develop mastery in that area.

Continued direction also reduces the level of autonomous experience in their role. We leave no room for them to influence or contribute to the process. As a result they will feel less satisfied with the work and less valued by you as a leader and by the organisation as a whole.

By not allowing your staff to develop autonomously, you also fail to help them to develop and build up their autonomy so that over time they can begin to influence and contribute to processes within the organisation. And when you don't facilitate this process, ultimately your team will lose the will to do either. They will lose the desire to even try.

It's at this point that intrinsic motivation is at its lowest. Instead of a team that is engaged and contributing to team and organisational goals with independence and initiative, you'll get staff who behave like mindless robots completely reliant on their leader to think for them and tell them what to do. And eventually your people will become so dissatisfied in the workplace that they begin actively looking for opportunities elsewhere.

It's kind of like the parent who does everything for their child. If a parent is the only one who ever cleans the room or cooks dinner, a child never learns the discipline of keeping the house tidy or how to cook for themselves. Importantly, they never even learn *why* it's important that those things get done. They grow into teenagers and young adults who are living at home, can only cook two minute noodles and are happy to live in the middle of piles of mess while their parents bemoan the fact that they never take responsibility for themselves and their lives.

While many of us might be able to relate to this, most of us would describe this situation (at least in part) to be a result of bad parenting rather than a lack of character in the child. The parent hasn't prepared the child for adult life and hasn't fostered a sense of initiative and responsibility.

In most workplaces, it's really not that different.

Activating intrinsic motivation

According to self-determination theory three characteristics are the key components of intrinsic motivation.[6] These are a sense of mastery, a sense of autonomy and a sense of connectedness.[7]

Intrinsic motivation is vital in the workplace. This is the thing in humans that compels them to 'seek out novelty and challenges, to extend and exercise one's capacities, to explore, and to learn'[8]. As leaders we all want our teams to be filled with people who are intrinsically motivated in their work. People who are proactive, passionate and purpose driven. But so often our default approach as leaders undermines the very thing we desire in our people. We need to take steps to be intentional about fostering empowerment amongst our teams.

Empowerment is the increased ability to operate independently. It's characterised by increased autonomy and is associated with higher levels of intrinsic motivation. The science on the subject is pretty conclusive. In terms of intrinsic motivation, there is a significant link between employees' sense of psychological empowerment and a leader's empowering behaviour.[9]

One study conducted in 2010 is significant because it not only relates the empowering behaviours of leaders with intrinsic motivation, but also with employee creativity, focusing on creative problem-solving.[10] The study involved a survey of 498 professionals in the technology and software development industry where substantial creative problem-solving is required to be effective. They assessed four leadership behaviours:

1. Enhancing meaning (understanding contributions to the big picture)

2. Promoting participation (in decision-making)

3. Expressing confidence (in staff abilities to perform)

4. Providing autonomy.[11]

When leaders exhibited these four behaviours it increased the staff's sense of psychological empowerment, which in turn increased both the intrinsic motivation and the degree to which they engaged in the creative problem-solving processes. Empowered staff then were much better at identifying problems, searching for relevant information and generating potential ideas and solutions when encountering workplace problems.[12]

As leaders we all want to see more of these qualities – and these results – in our teams. And it all starts with empowering our staff.

So how do we ensure that we're doing that? By creating situations where we're coaching (asking) rather than directing (telling). And that's because asking activates potential.

Activating through empowerment

When I speak to leaders about empowering their staff, I talk about the three Es of empowerment:

1. Equip

2. Enable

3. Encourage

Equip

The first stage of empowering your staff is to *equip* them with the skills, knowledge and understanding they need to operate independently. This includes teaching and training as we introduce new skills. And it also means equipping them with the ability to identify skill and capability gaps, and the strategies and resources to address these gaps, both at an individual and an organisational level.

Enable

The second stage of empowering your staff is to *enable* them to perform, develop and pursue their potential. At the heart of this stage is really providing your people with the opportunities they need to improve and develop new skills and capabilities. It may be the opportunity to practice and improve their current skill sets. It might be the opportunity to participate and contribute to initiatives and assist in decision-making across the organisation. It also might be (and should be) the opportunity to influence their world of work and how they do that work.

Enabling this ongoing learning is a big part of providing autonomy at work and empowering staff.

Encourage

The final stage of empowering your staff is to provide *encourage*ment. This is important because it's how you build a sense of self-belief and self-confidence in your staff. If your people aren't confident in their ability to perform in a particular area, they won't be motivated to do so. And they'll only venture into that area of work when pushed.

However, as leaders, we want our staff to be self-motivated to try to develop more areas of skills and capabilities. We want them to have that all-important self-efficacy we discussed earlier.

Self-efficacy is vital. We know that our sense of self-belief is greatly increased when we are surrounded by others who believe in us. However, when we believe in ourselves and our ability to perform, we're much more likely to act independently and be proactive. Even better, we'll have greater satisfaction in our work.

Asking activates potential

As leaders we need to pursue the empowerment of our staff and this demands that we shift from directing and telling, to asking and coaching. Of course asking questions is by no means the only way to empower our staff. But it is an effective way to enhance other initiatives at each stage of the empowerment journey. By asking strategic questions we are teaching and guiding. But more importantly, we're also role modelling the ability to ask such questions of ourselves.

Strategic questions equip your staff with the foundations for strategic thinking. By asking questions you're also providing them with the opportunity to engage in the type of thinking that is required of leaders at the next level. You're providing them with the opportunity to identify, articulate and understand the bigger picture. And you're enabling a sense of autonomy and influence.

For an individual to really pursue and realise their potential, they need to be empowered to do so. Asking (and therefore coaching) is an invitation to do so.

Turning the ship around

One of the greatest stories of empowerment I know is shared in the book *Turn the Ship Around* by L. David Marquet[13]. Marquet was a US Navy captain, who studied for 12 months to take command of the highest-performing submarine in the US Navy, the *USS Olympia*.

In the US Navy the captain is the expert on the ship. If something goes wrong on a vessel, the captain is the one tasked with knowing how to fix it and gives the orders for people to do so. Three weeks before he was due to take command of the Olympia, Captain Marquet was instead ordered to take command of another vessel, the *USS Santa Fe*. Not only was it a completely different type of submarine, but it also happened to be the lowest-performing submarine in US naval history.

Marquet had spent 12 months preparing and becoming an expert for a completely different boat. In fact, the difference was so stark that very little of his preparation was relevant to commanding the *Santa Fe*. Because of this Marquet really was not the expert. He was unable to provide the level of direction that was traditional for a submarine captain. Doing so would have been dangerous, not only for the safety of the vessel, but also for the crew on board.

In this scenario Marquet had to rely on the competence of his crew in order to sail the submarine. So, the only way he could successfully command this vessel was by empowering his crew. While there were a number of strategies he used to do this, one of the key elements of his approach was to ask effective questions.

In his book Marquet outlined the 20 mechanisms he used to change culture and empower his crew. Many of these involved asking different types of questions in different scenarios. Some of his mechanisms, and the associated questions, were to:

1. **Resist the urge to provide solutions.** To encourage proactive problem-solving, he asked the crew, 'What do you think needs to be done to solve the problem?'

2. **Think out loud.** To stimulate other's thinking, he would share his own by asking a question such as, 'I wonder what the enemy would likely do in this scenario?'

3. **Stop briefing – instead certify.** Rather than telling people what was about to happen he would determine (or certify) that his team knew what they needed to do by asking, 'What needs to happen in order to achieve our goal?'

4. **Begin with the end in mind.** To make sure his crew remained outcome focused he would ask, 'What is the outcome we're trying to achieve here?'

This approach – built around the above methodologies (and others) and including asking strategic questions to empower and develop his crew – transformed the culture of the *Santa Fe*. And it produced incredible results. Morale increased significantly, as did engagement, retention and satisfaction amongst the crew.

Most tellingly, within three years the *Santa Fe*, once the lowest-performing boat in the Navy, received the highest performance rating in US naval history. Marquet was literally able to turn the ship around. And he did it through asking questions to empower his people.

Setting great leaders apart

The ability to empower others is often what sets great leaders apart from their peers. As John Maxwell, American author, speaker, pastor and leadership expert, writes, 'A leader is great not because of his or her power, but because of his or her ability to empower others'.[14]

This ability to empower others is only going to become more necessary for leaders and companies in the future. With the pace of technology development, the increase of information flow and the exponentially dynamic nature of the environment in which we operate, it's simply impossible for leaders to be across everything.

Gone are the days when a single individual could be the expert in every area of their business, the marketplace and their people. Today, more than ever, leaders and organisations need to empower their people to meet some of those levels of expertise. This is why, when describing the requirements of leadership in the future, Bill Gates says, 'As we look ahead into the next century, leaders will be those who empower others.'

Coaching vs mentoring

When I ask people to identify what they think coaching is, mentoring almost always appears on the list. Coaching and mentoring are often used interchangeably when talking about developing people, both in organisational policy and human resources literature. But they are two different things. And it is worth taking the time to distinguish between the two.

Mentoring

Mentoring is a process where one person, the mentee, leverages the subject matter expertise of another, the mentor. So someone looking for mentoring in a particular area will identify a person with both the expertise and experience in that particular area before approaching them to be their mentor. It is very unlikely and most probably unwise for someone to approach an individual who has no expertise or experience in the particular field of interest for mentoring.

As David Clutterbuck, one of Europe's most prolific authors and thinkers on management, writes, 'A mentor is a more experienced individual willing to share knowledge with someone less experienced in a relationship of mutual trust.'[15] The way mentors share this knowledge is by providing guidance and advice based on their expertise and experience.

Mentoring is like an explorer showing you the map of their own journey – where they went, what mountains they climbed and what rivers they crossed. It's about sharing how they faced those challenges and how they managed to get to where they are now. So, at the end of the day, the prerequisite to being a good mentor is having subject matter expertise in a particular field.

Coaching, however, is different.

Coaching

Remember coaching is the process of asking strategic questions. In a pure coaching environment, therefore, no advice or guidance is given. The coach only asks questions – so they don't necessarily have to have subject matter expertise.

I have coached F/A-18 Hornet jet pilots. But I have never sat in the cockpit of a fighter jet, let alone flown one. I have coached lawyers, but I've never set foot in a court of law. I have coached senior military commanders and I've only ever been trained to lead teams of 10 men on the battlefield. My success in each of those engagements was not based on my subject matter expertise, but on my knowledge of the coaching process and my experience applying it.

Understanding that coaching doesn't require subject matter expertise is actually quite liberating for leaders because it means that they don't have to have all the answers. When we, as leaders, feel like we have to have all the answers and provide all the guidance and advice for our people all the time, we place ourselves under an enormous amount of pressure.

Coaching skills allow us to help our team and our people find the answers when we don't have them ourselves. It also helps us to lead effectively across a wider range of circumstances and in a fast-changing environment. Coaching skills allow a leader to lead, influence and develop others in teams, departments or other areas of business in which they have no background.

The difference between mentoring and coaching

The difference between mentoring and coaching can be found in rock climbing. Mentoring is like an experienced climber showing someone the route they took to scale a cliff. It might even be handing them the rope they laid to help them complete the climb itself. Coaching, however, is helping the climber to pioneer their own route up the cliff and lay their own rope as they go.

When it comes to developing people it's important to understand that it's OK for leaders to mentor. In many situations it's vital. At the same time when we're mentoring, there is still a level of telling and directing. In other words, we're still doing the thinking for people.

However, as with any other leadership activity, mentoring can be enhanced with the use of coaching skills. By sharing their experiences and then asking the mentee to identify lessons and principles that might apply in their situation and what actions they might take in light of those insights, the mentor will still provide many of the benefits of coaching. This is why an Air Force colleague of mine, Air Commodore Ian Scott says, 'Good mentors will use coaching skills, but good coaches will never mentor.'

The great movie director Steven Spielberg once said, 'The delicate balance of mentoring someone is not creating them in your own image, but giving them the opportunity to create themselves.' It is coaching skills that allow leaders to mentor in this way.

Reflection time

1. How has your perception of coaching changed after reading this chapter?

2. What's your natural approach to dealing with problems and developing people?

3. How does that align or differ from coaching?

CHAPTER THREE

The benefits of coaching

'The job of the leaders as coach is to ignite the creative genius in your people, turn it into positive power and to use that power to create enthusiasm in the workplace that makes a real difference to the organisation.'
– Simon Lee

When it comes to trying to describe and quantify the benefits of coaching, there's no end to the studies and statistics that you can find on the internet. In fact, a single Google search for 'coaching research' results in about 345,000,000 results.

Of course when you dive down into the results, many of the statistics seem to be over-sensationalised. And the size of the impact appears almost too good to be true. Claims of coaching that led to millionaires. Or coaches who impacted every person they ever came into contact with.

What do they say about things that are too good to be true? They often are.

As a psychologist, I am a trained scientist – a scientist who studies people. So when it comes to the big, overblown statistics, I immediately begin to question the scientific rigour of the process undertaken to measure them. While many impacts described in these studies are consistent with more robust scientific studies, the size of the statistics is not.

In this section I will share some of the key benefits of coaching that have been identified by researchers in published, peer-reviewed scientific literature. This means that they are demonstrated and verifiable benefits – rather than simply anecdotal claims. I've also included a couple of benefits based on my own experience both as a coach and a leader. I hope this will give you more confidence in the *real* benefits leaders and their teams will achieve from introducing coaching into the workplace.

If you're already convinced about the benefits of coaching, feel free to skip to the next chapter!

Self-efficacy

One of the most prominent benefits of coaching is that it significantly boosts self-efficacy. (Remember that self-efficacy is defined as the belief that an individual holds about their ability to influence the world around them.[1]) This is demonstrated by many studies and one excellent analysis[2] of the results of 52 separate studies on coaching in the workplace. Improving self-efficacy is important because we also know that self-efficacy is responsible for a 28% increase in performance[3].

The fact that coaching improves people's self-efficacy, or self-belief, in their ability to achieve goals and make a difference makes sense. Coaching is all about assisting people to learn how to make positive changes in their world and their work. And self-belief is a key enabler of change that coaches seek to cultivate. So we would expect that self-belief would be developed by coaching.

When I was a teenager, my Dad and I went gliding. We took a holiday, stayed near an airfield and had five days filled with gliding lessons. My instructor, Gerhart, taught us how to take off by being towed behind a small plane. And, of course, how to land without crashing.

In between, while we were in the air, he taught us how to feel the wobble of the wings that indicated a thermal up-draft and how to position the aircraft to be lifted by the column of warm rising air. The result was the glider spiralled upwards, gaining altitude, going higher and higher. Gerhart was a semi-retired German with decades of gliding experience. He would constantly ask, 'Did you feel zat?', referring to the wobble of the wings indicating a new updraft.

Each flight we gained more experience, more confidence and more self-belief. Eventually we were able to take the joystick and fly the glider by ourselves. It was an experience I'll never forget. Thanks Dad!

There are many similarities between a leader who coaches and my gliding instructor. First, the gliding instructor was in the cockpit and in the same glider as me, just as a leader is in the workplace and on the same team as their staff. So, in both situations, they have skin in the game.

Second, they both teach, and then let go. My gliding instructor taught us how to fly and once we were able to do it on our own, let us find the updrafts and position the glider into an upwards spiral.

The coaching leader is much the same. Initially, they help their team learn how to solve problems, achieve goals and perform in the workplace. And once they've achieved it, let go and let them 'fly' on their own. Before long, the individuals and teams are in a self-perpetuating upwards spiral, rising to new heights of both confidence and performance.

Just like a glider spiralling on a thermal.

Self-awareness

Like self-efficacy, awareness in general and self-awareness specifically, is an important requirement for change and, therefore, one of the elements of the triune focus of coaching. Cultivating it is a focus of coaching, so it's no surprise that gaining an increase in self-awareness is also one of the benefits of coaching.

One study[4] was specifically designed to investigate whether or not coaching develops self-awareness. In this study, the researchers used 360-degree feedback assessments to measure a manager's level of self-awareness.[5]

The 360-degree feedback process compared 20 managers' self-assessments of their behavioural competency, interpersonal competency and their personal responsibility, with the staff's assessment of the manager's performance in these three areas. Lower discrepancies between self and staff ratings indicated higher levels of self-awareness (and higher discrepancies showed a lower level of self-awareness). Managers were then provided a coaching program at the end of which the 360-degree feedback process was repeated.[6]

At the start of the program, managers rated their own performance significantly higher than their staff did. At the end of the coaching program, there was no significant difference between the manager's self-ratings and those of their staff. Interestingly, the managers' self-ratings remained consistent both before and after the coaching program. It was the staff's assessment of their manager's performance that had increased.[7]

These results suggest two things. First, that the manager's performance increased because of the feedback-coaching combination. This is what led to the higher staff assessments.

Additionally, if performance increased without any change in manager self-awareness, we would expect managers to rate themselves higher at the end of the program than at the beginning. Because this didn't happen, we get our second understanding – that the managers actually became more aware of their real level of performance by realising that their original self-assessment was likely inflated. As a result, despite real increases in their performance, their self-assessment remained the same as originally.

While self-belief allows us to have the confidence to make the changes required to achieve goals, it is self-awareness that allows us to know what changes are required and how to make those changes. The greater our level of self-awareness, the more we understand what changes we can make to our own thinking and our own behaviour to get the outcomes we desire.

Great leaders understand that how they interact with their staff can significantly influence their levels of motivation, inspiration, satisfaction, commitment and overall performance at work. These leaders are self-aware enough to also know how they can influence their own behaviour in order to interact with their staff in a way that brings out the best in their teams. Coaching leaders not only possess this level of self-awareness, they seek to foster it in those they lead.

Satisfaction, organisational commitment and turnover intention

In the self-awareness study mentioned above, an increase in staff competency assessments was not the only evidence that coaching improved the managers' performance. As part of the study, levels of job satisfaction, organisational commitment and turnover intention for both managers and staff were also measured.[8] The results of the study showed that after the coaching program, levels of job satisfaction and organisational commitment were significantly higher for both managers and staff alike.[9] And for both cohorts, turnover intention was significantly lower.[10]

When you stop and think about it, this makes sense. Coaching helps people to solve problems, overcome challenges and achieve goals. As humans, achieving goals and solving problems is inherently satisfying. If we're able to do this on a regular basis in our work, of course, we're going to find our work satisfying. So, it's no wonder that the managers who were receiving coaching – and so achieving and solving – experienced greater job satisfaction.

Additionally, satisfaction creates commitment. When we experience satisfaction, we also experience something akin to a sense of gratitude which generally results in higher levels of commitment towards the source of the satisfaction. If the source of that satisfaction is work – well, it's the organisation who provides the work. And because of that, people begin to feel more commitment towards the organisation that gave them those feelings.

Job satisfaction and organisational commitment are both the result of, and contributors to, workplace performance. If a leader or manager has these, research shows they are likely able to perform at a higher level.[11] At the same time, if a leader's role is to achieve results through the performance of their team, their own performance as a leader is contingent on their ability to create an environment that promotes these same qualities in the people they lead. If they can do that, they create a healthy culture in their team and/or organisation. And a healthy culture is something people don't want to leave.

Self-belief and trust also reduce turnover intention

High levels of job satisfaction and commitment aren't the only indicators of a healthy culture. Trust is also a significant factor and an important part of staff retention.

Researchers Ladegard and Gierde studied the role of coaching in developing the self-belief of leaders and the impact this had on the levels of trust they were given by their teams.[12] The study consisted of two groups of leaders and their teams. One group received a six-month coaching program, while the second group acted as a control group.

At the end of the six-month coaching program, the level of self-belief in the leaders was significantly higher for leaders that received coaching compared with the leaders who did not. Importantly, the teams of the coaching cohort of leaders reported higher trust in their leaders and a reduced intention to leave the organisation.[13]

There's the old adage that people don't leave companies, they leave managers. And in my experience – and as the research proves – this holds true. But the reciprocal result is true as well. People stay at a company because of a good relationship with their manager or leader – not because of the company itself. In fact, it is sometimes surprising how much employees will endure if they have a trusting relationship with their immediate leader.

Trust is a valuable commodity. Just like satisfaction and commitment, trust is both a result of, and contributor to, leadership performance. And just like satisfaction engenders commitment towards its source, so trust inspires loyalty.

Loyalty has become more important than ever because reducing turnover has become more important than ever. In a world where the average organisational tenure continues to drop[14] and the ease with which staff can find new opportunities for work continues to increase[15], building healthy cultures that provide high-trust relationships, ensure job satisfaction and inspire organisational commitment needs to be a priority for every workplace.

Employee engagement

Healthy work cultures not only keep staff from leaving, they also keep them engaged in their work. The concept of workplace engagement was big in the 90s. So much so that one of the biggest companies in the HR analytics field, Gallup, built their entire business around it.

Gallup categorises employees as either engaged, not engaged or actively disengaged.[16] In fact, their 'technical term' for being 'miserable at work is actively disengaged'. On the other hand 'engaged employees' are highly involved in and enthusiastic about their work and workplace.[17] They are psychological 'owners' – the employees who drive performance and innovation and move the organization forward'.[18] Sounds good. That's what we want, right?

Unfortunately, in their State of the Global Workplace: 2022 Report, Gallup reports that the percentage of engaged employees in Australia and New Zealand was at a dismally low 17%.[19] That is a three point drop since 2020 and below the global average of 21%. And the pandemic is only a small part of the problem, as pre-pandemic engagement levels were reportedly only 22%.[20] (I do wonder what's going on in Nicaragua where engagement levels are at 63%!)

This lack of engagement has a real cost. In fact, Gallup estimates that the lack of engagement and the associated reduced productivity costs the global economy US$8.1 trillion each year.[21]

There's a desperate need for good leaders who can unlock the potential in their workforce and bring out the best in their staff.

These are leaders who can create a healthy work culture that leads to engaged employees. Luckily coaching helps here too.

Research published in 2014 examined the effect of a coaching program on workplace engagement across two Australian state police services.[22] The coaching program included both 360 feedback and individual coaching sessions and was delivered to a group of 70 leaders.[23]

The study found that the staff who worked directly for leaders who were participating in the coaching program had higher perceptions of workplace support and strategic alignment, which in turn produced significantly higher levels of workplace engagement. And these staff had greater levels of job satisfaction compared to the control group.[24]

I've seen this play out in the work of my own clients. One great example is a client in the disability support sector. As part of their work, they delivered mandatory clinical supervision sessions with support workers. The managers didn't enjoy delivering these, and generally only conducted them out of obligation. And the support workers didn't enjoy attending either.

The coaching program helped the organisation's managers transform these unloved mandatory sessions into coaching and mentoring sessions. And while it took a couple of sessions for the support workers to get used to the change in approach, gradually they became more and more engaged.

It wasn't long before the managers were receiving comments of gratitude and expressions of how much their people were enjoying the sessions and even looking forward to them. I even had one manager who had to delay these sessions with their staff tell me how much he missed them. Interestingly, the turnover rate among the support workers also dropped during this time.

It might be easy to look at the global engagement levels and become depressed. However, they also reflect the great opportunity currently available to leaders. Employee engagement could become a competitive advantage for your organisation. Coaching leadership could be the key to unlocking that opportunity.

Innovation

To innovate is to implement new ideas in order to make changes to something that is established. And while most people agree that you have to innovate to stay relevant in business, most people also don't like to make changes for the sake of change. In fact, they tend to stay in the status quo unless and until they encounter a problem. When they do, then they look at how to innovate. So, for practical purposes, innovation is all about solving problems.

Albert Einstein is famously quoted as saying (though perhaps erroneously), 'We cannot solve our problems with the same thinking we used to create them.' Whether Einstein said this originally, or the source is elsewhere, it doesn't change the fact that innovation is the way we change that thinking.

Of course, the best way to shift our thinking (and innovate our thought processes) is to ask different questions. In describing how information can change our perceptions and, therefore, our thinking, English anthropologist and social scientist Gregory Bateson is said to have described a piece of information as 'a difference that makes a difference.'

This is an apt description of great questions – they are in search of a difference that makes a difference. They search for a different perspective that creates a difference in our thinking, which in turn results in us taking a different course of action. That action is innovation.

Asking great questions is a core coaching skill and an excellent way to innovate. The coaching process helps people unlock and step away from their established ways of thinking about problems and explore different perspectives to identify new solutions. Whether they're aware of it or not, great innovators always use coaching skills.

In 2021, researchers in China studied the link between coaching leadership and innovations among employees.[25] Examining 88 leaders and their 292 team members, they found that the more a leader coached their team, the more likely the team was to both engage in innovation processes within the company and display innovative behaviours such as generating and implementing new ideas at work.[26]

During my time as part of the Air Force Leadership Coaching Program, I remember hearing a great example of how coaching improves innovation. Several years ago, there was a problem with the KC-30 multi-role tanker. This is the aircraft that the Australian, US, UK and other air forces around the world use for air-to-air refuelling. The problem had persisted for several years.

One day a young technician, who just happened to be the most junior member in his squadron, was complaining about the problem to his corporal. This corporal had just received coaching skills training and thought this might be an opportunity to develop his new skill set. He began to coach this junior technician, challenging him to identify the problem and brainstorm potential solutions that might solve the problem. Because of that conversation the junior technician identified a real solution to a problem that had been going on for years. This was ultimately sent up the chain, signed off on by the Deputy Chief of Air Force and implemented.

This is a fantastic example of coaching leadership in practice. The corporal was by no means an expert coach or even someone experienced in using coaching skills. Yet they had a go at using them and were able to meaningfully innovate in a way that solved an organisation-wide issue. The corporal was able to create an environment where innovation could take place and lead in a way that brought the best out of his team member. He did that using coaching skills.

Peter Drucker once said, 'The enterprise that does not innovate ages and declines. And in a period of rapid change such as the present … the decline will be fast.' While those words may have been uttered in the 20th Century, they are truer now than ever. As the requirement for companies to innovate grows, so does their need for coaching skills.

Boosts resilience and wellbeing

In one of the early versions of my Coaching Leader Program (the program after which this book is named), I was working with a leadership team who were all on the fast track to burn out. When I began working with the team, I had concerns about the wellbeing of each one of them. But by the end of the six-month program, my concerns had evaporated. They were motivated, felt less stress and pressure at work and were experiencing better health physically. All this despite an increase in workload due to the growth of the company and successes they had made. In fact, while their workload increased, so did their wellbeing.

Why? Well the coaching process, despite being designed to teach them coaching skills and coach them to coach their people, also taught them resilience. And this new resilience meant they were better able to manage under stressful circumstances.

Experiencing a boost in one's resilience as a byproduct of coaching is a phenomenon not unique to my own coaching programs. In fact in a 2015 study leaders were interviewed within 12 months of completing a coaching program.[27] The results from that study 'indicated that leaders did perceive coaching to have affected their resilience, even if this was not a defined objective for the coaching.'[28]

There were five themes that emerged from these interviews. These were:

1. Reclaiming self-belief
2. Learning
3. Seeing a wider perspective
4. Supportive relationships
5. Thinking space[29]

Re-establishing self-belief in one's ability to overcome challenges is an important contributor to resilience, as is the growth, development and perceived progress that comes with learning. Adopting multiple perspectives in order to find meaning in suffering and challenges also contributes to resilience, as do meaningful and supporting relationships. Thinking space allows one to develop plans, maintaining a sense of control in times of challenge, which is also an important element of resilience.

Another study that came out of the University of Sydney's Coaching Psychology Unit compared both the resilience and wellbeing of leaders who participated in a leadership coaching program, with a control group of leaders who didn't receive coaching.[30] Those that took part in the coaching experienced significant increases in resilience and wellbeing (with a corresponding reduction in depression scores) as well as higher levels of goal attainment and achievement.

There is also evidence to suggest that the wellbeing benefits of coaching are not limited to those leaders who receive coaching, but extend to the teams they lead as well. Another University of Sydney study used social network analysis to look at the effects of coaching experienced by those who interacted with those being coached.[31]

What the researchers found was that not only did the leaders who received coaching experience increased wellbeing, but so did those who worked closely to them. This study also demonstrated significant increases in goal attainment and transformational leadership in the leaders being coached.[32]

It is important to note that all three of the coaching programs mentioned here were not designed to target or develop resilience and wellbeing. Each of them was focused on developing leadership capability. However there were significant improvements in resilience and wellbeing in each case, as a natural byproduct of coaching.

The takeaway? Organisational leaders looking to improve their leadership capability by providing coaching can be confident that those who both receive coaching and coach their teams will receive these important additional benefits of increased resilience and wellbeing.

Emotional intelligence

Emotional intelligence is the ability of an individual to perceive, understand and use emotional information. So someone with high emotional intelligence has awareness of their own emotions and the ability to use that awareness to regulate their behaviour when experiencing strong emotions. They're also able to perceive emotions in others and respond in a way that allows them to manage those relationships and achieve the outcomes they want.

It's fairly self-evident that these are important abilities for any leader to cultivate. While many people seem to naturally develop emotional intelligence as they mature, others find it challenging. But it's a skill people can learn and develop.

The former director of the University of Sydney's Coaching Psychology Unit, Anthony Grant, measured the levels of emotional intelligence developed in leaders during a 13-week coaching skills training program.[33] He compared the data against a comparison group who attended only two days of workshops.

The results of that analysis are illuminating. Leaders who undertook the 13-week program experienced significant development in their levels of emotional intelligence, while the control group did not. This is not only evidence that emotional intelligence can be developed through coaching. It also demonstrates that leaders who learn to coach become more emotionally intelligent and, therefore, better leaders.

As Grant writes, 'Coaching skills are inextricably related to emotional intelligence.'

Coaching creates space

The 2015 study referred to earlier identified thinking space as one of the benefits of coaching that contributed to resilience and wellbeing.[34] Part of the reason this thinking space is so valuable is because it is so rare.

In a 2016 survey of over 6,000 people, 71% were interrupted frequently throughout their work day, and only 29% were able to actively block out distractions.[35] If that was the case in 2016, then how much worse is it today given our increased connectivity?

Most leaders fall prey to the busy-ness that comes as part and parcel of their roles as leaders. They're dealing with back-to-back meetings, constant interruptions, overflowing inboxes and never ending to-do lists. They don't have the time or space to think, to problem solve or to reflect.

When they're in this state, leaders often experience what I call the thought tornado. Because they are on the go all the time, their minds are constantly moving at a million miles an hour. Their thoughts are spinning around in circles so much that they can't identify which thoughts are beneficial and what knowledge is useful.

When we're in a thought tornado we also can't make the connections that lead to solutions. We need time and space to do that. Coaching provides this space. Dedicated coaching appointments provide uninterrupted time to slow down and focus on a particular issue. Even better, there's someone to help facilitate that reflection and thinking.

This time and space is precious. It allows for the necessary thinking required to solve root-cause problems rather than applying band-aid solutions on the run. It provides the opportunity to do the strategic work that allows leaders and teams to be proactive rather than reactive. It gives us the time to reflect on our experiences, to articulate the insights and lessons to be learned from them and consider how we might apply those lessons in the future.

Doing all this with a coach, or with a leader who coaches, can make the use of this time and space that much more meaningful. One of my favourite quotes which has been attributed to many different people is, 'Thoughts untangle themselves over the lips and through the fingertips.'

When we communicate our thoughts, whether speaking them out (over the lips) or writing them down (through the fingertips), we are forced to articulate our thoughts. It is this act of articulation that brings clarity. When we are being coached, we are asked questions that require us to think and then communicate our thoughts in order to answer the question. Thus the coaching process clarifies our thinking.

Coaching balances the brain

One of the key aims in coaching is to encourage people to unlock from their current perspective in order to view the circumstances and challenges they face in a different light. As a generalisation, when people think about a problem they are encountering, they will do so using either their left or right side of their brain.

The left side of the brain is associated with reason, logic and objectivity. It is where the processing of numbers and quantitative data happens. The right side of the brain is associated with emotion, creativity and intuition. It is where feelings, experiences and qualitative data are processed. Depending on their personality, training and life experience, people will develop a preference for thinking about problems with either their left or right side of the brain.

In and of itself, such a preference is not a problem. It can even be of great benefit and result in contributing to the individual's strengths and abilities, allowing them to excel in a particular area. However, as with any strength that is overplayed, it can derail us and get us stuck. When we encounter challenges and rely too much on a particular brain-sided thinking style, we lock on to a particular perspective and set of data, locking out different sets or types of data that may be relevant (remember the potato and straws?).

Consider Kathy, an accountant who loves numbers, systems and processes. She struggles to understand why her new office manager Jess doesn't want to implement a new customer relationship management tool (CRM) that collates customer data. Kathy knows that Jess is a people person, which is why she is so good at her job. They have discussed how the customer experience is one of Jess's top priorities, which is why her resistance to the new CRM is so confusing for Kathy. Logically, the more data you have about the customers, the more informed you are about how you can provide them with a great experience. It just doesn't make sense.

Kathy shares her frustration with Kevin, the business owner, who reminds Kathy about a recent team development day where Jess had shared that she had failed maths in school. He then asked, 'How do you think the prospect of making decisions using numbers and percentages is likely to make Jess feel?' Kathy has a light bulb moment as she considers how asking Jess to make decisions about customers based on data is likely to make her feel inadequate.

Kevin's question helped Kathy unlock her focus on the numbers, logic and left-brained thinking. She was able to think with the right side of the brain and consider the qualitative data of Jess's internal experience.

Kathy was able to set up a traffic light system within the CRM, so Jess didn't have to interpret numbers in order to utilise the customer data. The result was that Jess overcame her resistance and became a strong advocate for the implementation of the CRM across the business.

As leaders, we want our people to be able to figure out a way to overcome the challenges they face and to make informed decisions in the way that they do so. When our team brings us a problem, it is important to listen to how they are framing the problem, identifying what side of the brain they are thinking with and what type of data they are using to inform their perspective.

For those focused on logic and reason, it can be useful to consider the emotional experiences involved. For those focused on emotions and experiences, it can be useful to quantify those experiences so they can be analysed. By asking questions that encourage them to use a different part of their brain and consider different types of information, we can often facilitate a flash of insight that will help them overcome their immediate challenge.

Note: As a psychologist and professional, I feel bound to tell you that what I have just written is technically wrong. People do not think with either their left or right side of the brain at any one time. Nor are our left and right sides of our brains exclusively dedicated to logical or emotional processing, respectively. People think by activating different systems and regions across their brain and these systems often span brain hemispheres.

However, neuroscience is complicated stuff. I could talk to you about the perirhinal cortex, the prefrontal cortex, the premotor cortex, the primary motor cortex and the somatosensory cortex – and those aren't even all the cortexes! I could be technically accurate in describing how it all works, but it would be confusing and there would be nothing gained.

A friend of mine and fellow psychologist Dr Justin Coulson once gave me a piece of advice: 'It's better to be useful than to be right.' With this in mind, I acknowledge that this passage is an oversimplification to the point of being technically inaccurate. But I hope it's a useful way for leaders to think about how to use coaching skills to help their people.

Bring people on the journey

When I left the military full-time, I was a patrol commander, trained to lead teams on combat missions. I enjoyed the challenge of leadership and the opportunity to develop others and drive them towards achieving a common goal. So it wasn't long before I found myself in a civilian leadership position.

This position involved heading up a new team of volunteers who would be running community events for people in our own age group. Working with my up-line we pulled together a dozen really good people to form the team. These were individuals with great abilities who were good with people.

As a student of leadership, I knew what I had to do. I had prepared a vision statement, set goals, outlined expectations and developed a plan for the first few months. I felt I'd done the work and was ready. After all, how hard could it be? I was trained to lead men in combat – a far more difficult scenario. Leading a bunch of civvies couldn't be that hard.

I was about to learn a very difficult lesson.

While the launch night didn't go as smoothly as I'd planned I still came away feeling like it was a success. However a month later, I hung up the phone after having the final remaining member saying they no longer wanted to be part of the team. It had taken me about four weeks to lose an entire team of 15 people.

While this experience taught me a number of significant lessons, one of the biggest was the importance of bringing people on the journey. I failed to do that with this team. Instead I jumped straight into directing – 'this is what we are going to achieve' and 'this is how we're going to do it' and 'this is who is going to do what'. All the directing simply ended in disaster.

Of course, this isn't an unusual problem. After all, leaders spend much of their time thinking about setting direction and solving problems to enable their team to do what they need to. The team members, on the other hand, spend their day executing and doing the work. When it comes to directions, plans or solutions, the leader has already gone on that thought journey. So sharing can often become an afterthought.

But leaders need to be mindful that their team is yet to take that journey. If a leader wants to get their team to buy into their course of action and avoid resistance or losing their team as I did, they need to take them on that same thought journey.

Taking your team on your thought journey

By asking your team a series of strategic questions, you, as a leader, invite them to wrestle with the same considerations you did and, hopefully, arrive at the same conclusions. Because they have now arrived at the same conclusions themselves, they will have greater understanding, ownership and investment in the direction you want the team to travel in moving forward.

This is the difference between someone who is sharing their own journey of climbing Mt Everest, compared with someone retelling that climber's journey. The person who has actually taken the journey to the top of the world is going to be much more passionate and emotionally invested in the story. They will also be much more motivated to help others take that same journey.

When leaders share directions, plans and solutions with their teams, they help their team to be motivated and own both the process and the outcome. They also create the opportunity for their team to go and inspire *their teams* in the same way. Using coaching skills to facilitate a thought journey is one of the most effective ways a leader can achieve this.

Coaching softens the hard edges

Similar to how taking people on a journey creates a more vulnerable and open team, coaching skills soften the hard edges that driven, results-focused leaders often have. For many leaders, a focus on results and getting things done has led to their initial success. And it's the thing that's allowed them to rise to a leadership position.

However these qualities often result in leaders being task focused to the extent that they lose sight of the effects on people. As a result, their communication can become hard – short, sharp and blunt. These leaders are then failing to demonstrate the 'soft-skills' that are so important to effective leadership. This was a big part of my problem when I lost my team.

Imagine hammering plastic tent pegs into the ground using a metal hammer. What will the result be?

I recently went camping by a lake and because of the sandy soil I had to use plastic sand pegs when setting up our campsite. As I was hammering these sand pegs in using a standard hammer with a metal head, I misjudged the angle of the hammer swing. Rather than hitting the peg at just the right angle to drive it into the ground, I hit the side of the peghead. This resulted in bits of plastic chipping off the pegs and, ultimately, breaking completely. Eventually I realised the problem (besides my poor aim) and I switched to a mallet with a softer rubber head. I damaged no more pegs after that.

Switching from a metal hammer to a rubber mallet still allowed me to achieve the same goal, driving the peg into the ground. However, I did so without damaging the pegs. In the same way, using coaching skills and asking questions softens a leader's communication and leadership. It allows a leader to still pursue goals, achievement and performance, but in a way that doesn't damage people, relationships and culture.

Let's look at some examples.

- **When dealing with underperformance:** 'That's not good enough,' vs 'Do you think that meets the expected standard?'

- **When dealing with interruptions:** 'Go away,' or 'Now's not the time,' vs 'When do you think the best time to discuss this would be?'

- **When seeking process improvement:** 'Go and fix the process,' vs 'How could the team find ways to improve this process?'

- **When holding people accountable:** 'I saw you do this,' vs 'What do you think I observed?' Or, 'You said you were going to do this,' vs 'What was it you said you were going to do?'

As a leader you need to drive performance and push your people to achieve results. If you can't do that then you aren't a good leader. However, if you want to ensure your ability to achieve results through people sustainably and, therefore, perform as a leader over time, you need to be able to do that in a way that doesn't damage the relationships you have with those you lead.

Using coaching skills to ask strategic questions helps you to soften your communication to ensure both performance and relationships are maintained.

Initiative and proactivity

One of the biggest frustrations I hear from leaders is the lack of initiative displayed by their staff. 'I just wish my people were more proactive,' is something I hear a lot. And that's because it is a common challenge.

How traditional leadership approaches foster a reliance on leaders and stifle initiative has been discussed earlier in this book. As has how the shift from telling to asking can break that cycle and result in higher levels of proactivity. And this is backed up by research as well.

There was a study conducted in a large teaching hospital where a cohort of frontline nursing managers participated in a workplace coaching program.[36] The program included coaching seminars as well as group and individual coaching. At the completion of the six-month program, the nursing managers demonstrated significantly more proactive behaviours than prior to the coaching program. There were also increases in core role performance, self-awareness, wellbeing and goal attainment.[37]

Coaching and performance

Some of you reading this may be thinking, I've read all of these benefits but I haven't seen anything about the primary purpose for which coaching is employed in the workplace – to improve performance. While performance is a multi-faceted concept that can be hard to measure at times, there is plenty of evidence throughout the literature that both directly and indirectly demonstrates that coaching does improve performance.

Direct evidence can be found in many studies. One published in 2021 studied the effects of coaching on 170 employees of small to medium enterprises.[38] It found that coaching directly improved the performance of employees. It also found that coaching increased organisational citizenship behaviours, including being proactive and going above and beyond for the good of the company, which in turn also improved employee performance.[39]

In addition to the direct evidence, much of what you have read in this chapter provides indirect evidence of the relationship coaching has to both individual and organisational performance. Many of the studies included here have found increases in goal attainment due to coaching. And performance is often driven by and measured against the attainment of goals.

The qualities of self-efficacy and self-awareness are usually precursors to and correlates of a leader's performance. The concepts of job satisfaction, organisational commitment, employee engagement, trust, wellbeing and resilience are all qualities that a high-performance leader is both experiencing and fostering in their teams. Leaders who cultivate these qualities create environments that promote performance and bring out the best in the people they lead. If coaching contributes to and significantly improves each of these performance indicators, then a leader who coaches will significantly improve their performance, and that of their team.

The deciding factor – attitude

While the scientific research supports all of the benefits listed in this chapter, there is no guarantee that a leader who either receives coaching or coaches their people will experience all or even some of them. In my experience there is one factor that will determine whether or not coaching is beneficial. That factor is attitude.

I recall one coaching program where I was coaching several executives. While the majority of these executives actively engaged in the process, there was one who did not. He was willing to attend and discuss topics of concern, but he was not interested in engaging in the level of reflection that would provide insight and learning and result in expanding his self-awareness. Nor was he willing to take the action required to make improvements to his leadership or the performance of his company.

For this individual, there was no benefit derived from the coaching he received. And that came down to his attitude.

Both the leader who is coaching and the individual (or team) being coached have to be willing to engage with, and invest in, the coaching process. If they are not, they won't get those benefits.

Do the benefits of coaching last?

This chapter started by referencing a meta-analysis of 52 coaching studies[40] and it is here I'd like to return as we bring this chapter to a close. One of the most important questions to ask of any learning and development initiative is will the benefits last? Once a leader stops receiving coaching, will the benefits they and their team receive disappear?

After looking at all the evidence in the literature and the results of the 52 studies included in their research, the authors of the meta-analysis arrived at a promising conclusion. While they identified the need for much more research on the long-term effects of coaching, they wrote, 'the majority of these findings have been positive and support long-term sustained influence of coaching.'[41]

Coaching is not just about helping individuals to learn, but also how to learn. It is about equipping individuals to achieve their goals, solve their problems and overcome their challenges using their own abilities.

Coaching also helps individuals see how their learning in one area of work and life can be applied in other areas. In effect, coaching is as much about individuals learning the coaching process as it is about them achieving results from the coaching process. Once they learn the process, they are able to apply that process repeatedly with themselves and with others as required in the future. In that way, the benefits of coaching can not only be sustained in individuals who receive coaching, but replicated in those they coach.

Reflection time

1. Which of these benefits is most important to you as a leader?

2. Which would you like to see your team experience?

3. What would experiencing these benefits do for you and your team?

CHAPTER FOUR

What is a coaching leader?

'I could command in 15 minutes a day.
The rest of my time was coaching.'
– General Jim Mattis

It would be simple to assume that the term 'coaching leader' is simply the combination of its two elements – coach and leader – and surmise that a coaching leader is simply a leader that coaches. While in a very limited sense this is true, a 'coaching leader' is actually so much more.

To fully understand all that lies behind the title of 'coaching leader' it's important to understand what's wrapped up in those two components. The first three chapters of this book should give you a high-level understanding of what coaching is, and the next three will help you understand how it is applied. This one brings them together by taking us through what a coaching leader is.

First, let's take a bit of a look at what's really behind the concept of leader. There are thousands of different definitions of what a leader and leadership is. But all of them, in some way, boil down to a version of the following:

> Leadership is influencing a group of people towards a common goal.

Leadership is change

At the heart of leadership is the concept of change.

Let's consider the most basic leadership task – leading a person from point A to point B. For a leader to successfully complete this task there are two important changes that need to happen. First, the individual must have a change of behaviour, and second, they must have a change in location.

The individual being led started at point A and changed location to end up at point B. That individual started out as stationary and was required to move in some way in order to change their location. So, that first change is behavioural – and it is necessary to achieve the outcome. Once the behavioural change is underway (the person is moving) then the second change can occur (the location). And this achieves the ultimate outcome.

If you think of any leadership task, it is always about creating a change in order to get a positive outcome. This is the crux of the difference between leadership and management. While leadership is constantly pursuing change, management seeks to provide stability.

Every organisation needs structures, systems and processes in order to support its people and achieve its mission, purpose and vision. So, there needs to be a stable foundation upon which and within which people can operate in order to perform at their best. If things are constantly changing without structure and without some stability they eventually collapse.

It is the role of management to provide that stability and support by maintaining the structure and systems. And then, within that stable structure, leaders can pursue the change that will drive better outcomes for staff, teams and the organisation as a whole.

The functions of leadership and management are different, but both are needed in a successful organisation. And good leaders also need good management skills, while good managers also need to have the ability to influence and inspire change.

To what leadership style does the coaching leader belong?

So if leadership is influencing a group of people towards a common goal then the difference between leadership styles simply comes down to how leaders choose to influence their people. This could be transactional leadership, transformational leadership, authentic leadership, situational leadership, servant leadership, ethical leadership or even coaching leadership. Each of these require a specific set of skills and characteristics that the leader will use in order to influence their people and create the desired change.

The coaching leader uses a leadership style that relies heavily on coaching skills as the primary method for influencing change. This style of leadership sits under the broader style of transformational leadership.

Transformational leadership and the coaching leader

Transformational leadership is defined as:

> *a process that changes and transforms people. It is concerned with emotions, values, ethics, standards and long-term goals. It includes assessing followers' motives, satisfying their needs, and treating them as full human beings. Transformational leadership involves an exceptional form of influence that moves followers to accomplish more than what is usually expected of them.*[1]

So transformational leadership, in a nutshell, is leading in a way that transforms people into better versions of themselves. Coaching is a skill set inherent in all transformational leaders because it's a vital part of helping others to improve, and to continue to improve themselves over time.

It's also articulated as one of the core skills of transformational leadership models – for example, the Full Range of Leadership Model.[2] The coaching leader is one who is intentional about using coaching as a primary mechanism to lead and influence their people to make the changes required to achieve results, growing and developing them in the process.

The journey of a coaching leader

Becoming a coaching leader who meets both the criteria of being able to coach their team, and helping the team learn to coach others, means going through a journey of five stages.

The coaching leader's journey

	ACTIVITY	FOCUS	VALUE GENERATED	PERFORMANCE FACTOR
5	INSPIRING COACHING CULTURES	KAIZEN	100	10x
4	COACHING OTHERS TO COACH	EMBEDDING	75	5x
3	COACHING OTHERS	SKILLSET	50	3x
2	BEING COACHED	PRACTICE	10	1x
1	LOST	AWARENESS	-10	-5x

Level 1: The lost leader

The journey of a coaching leader begins with a lack of awareness. And leaders who lack awareness are lost.

There are two types of lost leaders. First, there are those who are so focused on themselves they disregard opportunities to develop others. Second, there are those that want to help others develop, but just don't know how.

Lost leaders: Type 1

The first type of lost leader – those who are so focused on their own abilities that they disregard opportunities to develop others – generally aren't even aware of the negative impact this has on their team. Instead, they are overconfident in and overreliant on their ability and often fall prey to the Dunning-Kruger Effect (a cognitive bias where people with limited knowledge or competence in an area greatly overestimate their own abilities in that area).[3]

One study in a leading software engineering company showed that 42% of developers self-estimated their own performance as being in the top 5% of the company[4]. Of course, this is a statistical impossibility. But this type of overestimation of ability is typical of 'lost' leaders. As Charles Darwin put it, 'Ignorance more frequently begets confidence than does knowledge'.

Type one lost leaders are often ignorant not only of what good leadership looks like, but also of the reality of the quality (or lack thereof) of their own leadership. In this way, they aren't that different from the old story of the frog in the well.

The frog who lives at the bottom of the well sees the round patch of sky above the well and believes that this is the whole world. It knows nothing of the mountains, the oceans or the world beyond. And because it has everything it needs at the bottom of the well (for the time being), like bugs to eat and water to drink and stay cool, it never needs to seek beyond the obvious.

These lost leaders are the same. They can't see what's beyond their limited view, and are often not even aware of their need for development. Sometimes they aren't even aware of what coaching is. They believe they already have everything they need, and so they fail to see the opportunities to coach others.

Lost leaders: Type 2

The second type of lost leaders are those that want to develop others but don't know how. They inadvertently reinforce reliance rather than foster independence, initiative and interaction. This isn't down to a lack of awareness or a lack of desire or even a lack of ability.

Instead, they're simply perpetuating the poor leadership that was role modelled to them. So, when they do try to help their people, they're stymied. It's like they're trying to remove a speck from someone else's eye when they have a log sticking out of their own.

The reality is, in both cases, lost leaders often do more harm than good. They create a poor experience for the people they lead and fail to create an environment that brings out the best in people. Their teams stagnate, and people languish as they struggle to produce the desired levels of performance without a leader who can show them the way to do so. Ultimately this results in driving people away from the company. These leaders fail to provide value to the company and end up detracting from its overall performance.

Level 2: Being coached

Let's go back to our little frog in the well story. Imagine now that the well dries up, the bugs leave and the frog, who is very hungry and thirsty, realises that it will need to do something if it wants to survive. It realises that it'll need to hop to the top of the well to see what it can see. When he does so, he looks over the top of the well and realises there's a whole world out there, with trees, flowers, marshes, ponds and more.

In the same way, once a leader realises their own gaps, they'll become aware of their own need for development. External feedback now becomes vital in order to raise awareness about themselves and their leadership that they cannot see. In order to access this world, they need to be willing to be coached themselves. It will open them up to seeing the larger world that is available to them.

Once a leader can see the areas that need work, they can be intentional about working on these areas. Their performance improves as they learn how to be more proactive in solving their own problems and by practising the leadership skills developed during their own coaching.

I remember in my first semester of university I did a subject on interpersonal communication. As part of that subject we had to receive feedback on how we communicate. And as a result of the feedback I became aware that I had a habit of finishing people's sentences because I was already formulating my response before they'd even finished speaking. Combined with my direct communication style this meant that I often came across as overconfident and sometimes even arrogant.

I realised that I wasn't truly listening to people. Simon Sinek says, 'Hearing is listening to what is said. Listening is hearing what isn't said'.[5] I was hearing but I wasn't *listening* because I was listening to respond rather than listening to understand.

Even once I became aware of this habit it was something that took me several years and a lot of hard work and intentional effort to break. To this day I am conscious and intentional of letting people finish what they have to say before I respond in a conversation.

By being coached and developing their own leadership skills, leaders will begin to do more good than harm. They'll also increase their own performance, effectiveness and, ultimately, the value generated for the organisation as a whole.

Level 3: Coaching others

Being coached teaches a leader both how to develop themselves, and the value of coaching in general. So once they have developed a *realistic* confidence in their own abilities, they can begin to shift the development focus from themselves to others.

This shift is not dissimilar to going from studying education to stepping into the classroom and teaching for the first time. As a leader you have to go from being coached, to being the coach. But the key to success at this stage is just as much about what you don't do as it is about what you do do. As John Whitmore said, 'As I and so many others have found, learning to coach is easy; it's giving up old habits that is the harder thing to do.'[6]

My tendency to begin formulating my response in my head while another person was still speaking was one of those bad habits.

Successful coaching is just as much about overcoming bad habits that inhibit good coaching, as it is about learning how to use good coaching skills and habits. This stage is often the longest on a coaching leader's journey and requires the hardest work. In many ways we are effectively rewiring our brain. That takes time, effort and intentionality.

But it is possible to move through this stage more quickly. In fact, there are two steps leaders can take to speed up their development.

Step 1: The first is by preparing to coach. This involves sitting down daily and identifying what opportunities to coach exist throughout the day. Once you've identified each opportunity, determine the key coaching skills required and some of the questions that might be relevant.

Step 2: The second step is to reflect on the coaching experiences you've had. As John Maxwell says, 'Reflection is the process that turns experience into insight.'[7] By reflecting on how you have been coached you are better able to identify and articulate what worked (and perhaps what didn't) and fuse those into your own coaching capabilities. This also helps you to consistently improve so you can make changes next time round.

Being disciplined with this approach of step one, preparing to coach, and step two, reflecting on your coaching experiences, is in itself an application of coaching skills. It is a form of self-coaching that will expedite your personal growth and development.

Level 4: Coaching others to coach

Once a leader has successfully learned to coach others, the next level of progression is to make the transition to coaching others to coach. This typically occurs when leaders are leading other leaders (but it's not always the case).

When this occurs, the coaching leader is now equipping leaders with the skills necessary to develop those they lead. This is where the benefits of coaching – and so the benefits to your team and organisation – begin to multiply. Consider – while a single teacher can teach a class of 20 students, equipping 10 teachers to each be able to teach their own class of 20 students results in 200 students being taught. The same is true in your own team.

A force multiplier

Once a leader is coaching others to coach, coaching skills become a force multiplier within the organisation. In the military, a force multiplier is something that is able to multiply an effect during operations. For example, a soldier with a rifle can only fire 30 rounds at the enemy before they are required to reload. A machine gun, however, has a faster rate of fire with the ability to link hundreds of rounds together, allowing continual fire. In this case the machine gun is a force multiplier, multiplying the amount of force one individual can employ against the enemy.

Another example is the air-to-air refuelling capability provided by the Air Force's KC-30 aircraft. The ability to refuel fighter jets mid-air multiplies the distance those jets can travel and the time they can stay in the air before having to return to refuel.

When a coaching leader is able to equip their team with coaching skills, they create a team of coaching leaders. And a team of coaching leaders are able to lead more effectively and develop organisational capability organically, and, in effect, multiply leadership within the organisation. The focus of this level has shifted from developing and practising the coaching skill set to embedding it within the psyche of their leaders, their culture and their ways of working with the team.

Do you recall my client in the disability sector that changed the nature of their clinical supervision sessions into coaching sessions? Their return from the coaching program was incredible. The managers took these skills and applied them enthusiastically and successfully, drastically changing the way they interacted with frontline staff. They even changed the name of their one-on-one supervision sessions to coaching and mentoring sessions.

But the change wasn't just seen in the name of the sessions and the success wasn't just at the organisational level. The organisation also used these coaching tactics proactively. Within their recruitment process, an integral part of the on-boarding and training of new junior supervisors by the middle managers was the use of coaching skills. This means that as these new supervisors interacted with the frontline staff they were doing so using a coaching approach, developing people while ensuring quality of service. And it was a great success. Today layers of leaders continue to be developed organically.

Level 5: Inspiring coaching cultures

The pinnacle of the coaching leader's journey is when they get to inspire coaching cultures. This goes beyond coaching others to coach, and expands it to encompass the culture as a whole. At this level coaching leaders are not just thinking about how they improve their own skill set or even how they develop and embed that skill set within a team. These leaders are combining coaching skills with strategic thinking and considering how to unlock that potential across the organisation.

Kaizen

The focus here is really applying the concept of *kaizen*. The concept of kaizen was popularised with the 2011 book, *The Toyota Way to Lean Leadership* written by Jeffery Liker and Gary Convis.[8] In this book, the authors outlined many of the concepts and principles that led to Toyota's sustained success in the automobile industry. One of these concepts was the philosophy of kaizen.

Kaizen is a philosophy of continuous improvement through personal development. However, the philosophy goes beyond this concept. True kaizen involves influence beyond borders and boundaries.

A coaching leader champions both coaching and the use of coaching skills by leaders across the organisation. They not only seek to continually improve the skill sets and performance within their team and department, but will also look for opportunities to have the same influence across the life of the company as a whole. While not looking to override the leadership of other teams they will be mindful of creating and leveraging opportunities to collaborate and interact with other teams, encouraging people to use coaching skills to enhance collaboration and reinforce a coaching culture.

An example of a coaching leader is Group Captain Simon Sauer. Simon was a successful military commander in the Air Force before discharging and taking a role for several years as CEO for the ex-services organisation Mates4Mates. Simon now spends a significant amount of his time as a reservist, actively sharing his wisdom and developing capability in a number of different areas across the Air Force.

Simon first came across coaching when he participated in the Air Force Leadership Coaching program. It was here that he was first trained in the use of coaching skills as a leader. The coaching process resonated with him so much that he became an accredited coach. Today, he remains a sought-after mentor who coaches many new commanding officers and other senior military commanders.

But Simon's work goes beyond just the individuals that he works with. He continues to operate across a wide variety of units within the Air Force and there are many commanders who would attribute their ability to successfully navigate leadership challenges and lead in a more effective manner to the coaching they received from Simon.

But more telling is that as a result of working with Simon, many of these commanders regularly seek out coaching skills training for their personnel as well. They understand the value that it holds on both a personal and organisational level. And after working with Simon, each of these leaders are not only more adept at developing people but also at encouraging the personnel they lead to use their coaching skills on a daily basis.

It's easy to think that in order for a coaching leader to coach others to coach as well, they need to be in a senior executive role that allows them to operate across multiple parts of the business. While often leaders who champion coaching do find themselves in such roles, it's not a prerequisite to operate at that level. In the same way, middle managers aren't limited from using coaching methods within their role requirements. In fact, they may also have the opportunity to influence and inspire coaching cultures outside their own teams if they are intentional about creating and leveraging opportunities to do so.

Sattar Bawany, a master executive coach and expert on leadership development and transitions, writes, 'A coaching culture all starts with a leader's willingness to engage in a coaching relationship and undertake reflection in order to develop themselves and others'.[9] All it takes is one passionate coaching leader achieving results in their own patch and others will come calling, opening the door for expanded influence.

The makeup of a coaching leader

So what makes a coaching leader? What is it that makes them different from the typical coach, or the typical leader?

As the model below shows, being a coaching leader consists of three primary components – the coaching mindset, the coaching skill set and the coaching practice. In this chapter we provide a brief summary and then subsequent chapters will delve into each in detail.

The coaching leader makeup

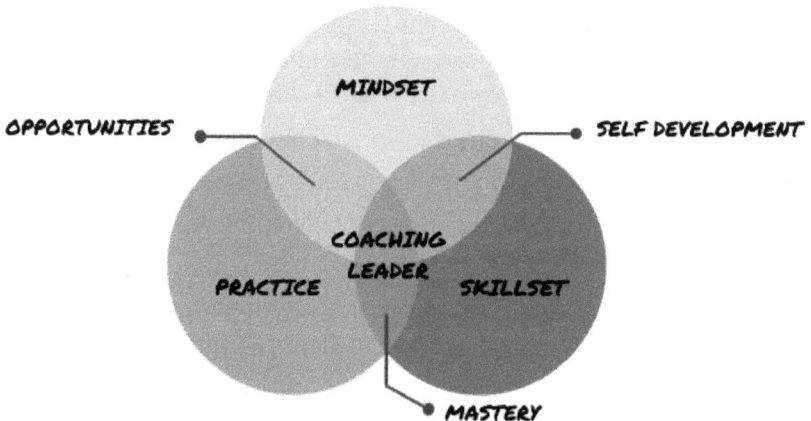

The coaching mindset

The coaching mindset incorporates more than just a good understanding of what coaching is and how it can be used effectively. It includes cultivating a growth mindset – a belief in people, their potential and their ability to make a difference.

People are more brilliant than they realise. Sometimes they just need help to realise it.

The coaching skill set

The coaching skill set is the suite of tools, methods and skills that enable a leader to coach. The more advanced a leader's skill set, the more enhanced their approach, and the broader the range of circumstances that they can impact.

The coaching practice

The coaching practice refers to the leader's application of coaching in the workplace. It refers to the disciplined development of their expertise in using coaching to enhance their leadership.

Together these three elements allow leaders to identify opportunities to coach and to self-coach in a way that consistently enables them to continue their own personal growth and development and eventually master the use of coaching as a leader.

The interactions

In any venn-diagram, I always get interested in the intersections. The intersections of this model produce opportunities, self development and mastery. When leaders have a coaching mindset and approach their leadership as a practice, they become aware of the opportunities that are available to coach. When they have the right mindset and a coaching skill set, they are continually self-coaching and growing themselves. Self-development is the result. So, when leaders continually practice applying their coaching skill set to their leadership, new levels of mastery are attained.

You're not an executive coach

It's important to remember that in the pursuit of becoming a *coaching leader*, we are not aiming to become an executive coach. Executive coaches prioritise developing people over everything else. They spend hours and dedicate large amounts of time, effort and attention in order to hone their ability and develop expertise into building people. This is their only goal.

As a leader, you cannot be this type of coach. The pressures of organisational leadership require your attention, focus and energy to be spread across a large number of areas – including developing your people. You will also need to drive performance and execute strategy. You will need to create and meet KPIs. And much more.

So, as a leader, you will have competing priorities to balance. And part of this is balancing the development of your people against the requirements of the organisation. You simply cannot dedicate the time and energy to honing your coaching skills to the same degree as an executive coach.

You can think of it like this – a surgeon who becomes the head of the medical school is rarely the most skilled surgeon in a hospital. Given their role as a teacher, they must attend to those teaching responsibilities. They have to prepare lessons, answer questions and even have office hours. Because of this they spend less time operating on patients, and maintaining and developing those skills and expertise. These are the 'executive coaches'.

On the other hand, there are many 'teaching' surgeons who do this as part of their role, but not their whole role. These are those that are in the operating room with residents, and who are overseeing and correcting their technique and helping them to increase their skills. Their job isn't to solely focus on creating other surgeons, but to help those surgeons within their reach to become *better* surgeons. These are 'coaching leaders'.

Coaching leaders aren't always expert coaches but they use coaching skills in order to develop capability and become expert leaders.

Reflection time

1. What aspect of being a coaching leader is most attractive to you?

2. If you were honest with yourself, what level would you be at on the coaching leader's journey?

CHAPTER FIVE

Mindset

'Each person holds so much power within themselves that just needs to be let out. Sometimes they just need a little nudge, a little direction, a little support, a little coaching – and the greatest things can happen.'
– Pete Carroll, NFL coach

One of the beautiful things about Paris and the surrounding French countryside are the long avenues of trees along many of the roads throughout France. The story goes that Napoleon wanted the trees planted along the road so his troops would be able to march in the shade throughout France. When he initially suggested the idea one of his officers challenged him saying it would take decades before any of the trees would be large enough to provide shade. To which Napoleon reportedly replied, 'Then we have no time to lose. We must plant today!'

In many ways, cultivating a coaching mindset is like growing a tree. A tree is strong and fruitful, but it takes a while to grow. There are aspects that like roots provide a strong foundation for thinking. And there are key beliefs that like branches, spread out and connect to each leaf (or thought).

PEOPLE HAVE
THE ABILITY TO
OVERCOME

EMPOWERED
WORKFORCE

PEOPLE
MATTER

ME FIRST,
THEN OTHERS

MINDSET

LONG TERM FOCUS   GROWTH MINDSET

Long term focus

The reality is that just like growing trees, coaching is a long term investment. As with all learning, growth and development the most significant benefits occur over time. In so many ways the modern world is oriented towards the short term. There are many contributing factors such as the advancement of technology and the speed with which life now occurs. We no longer have to wait for a dial-up connection to access the internet. Cooking with microwaves takes a matter of minutes. Streaming means your favourite TV show is available 24 hours a day. And in the business world, daily trading on the stock market gives real-time visibility and reporting of stock prices.

Each of these, and our world in general, promotes thinking about the short term rather than the long term even when it comes to impacts on organisational health, performance and sustainability. Such an orientation towards short-term thinking is in part why so many leaders rely on telling. Because it's quick, it's easy and, in most cases, the results are immediate. Realising the benefit of shifting to asking however takes time.

Coaching is like gardening

I consider myself a bit of a gardener and enjoy spending time in my veggie patch. It's one of the things that helps me relax and detach from my work on weekends. But gardening takes time. A gardener has to prepare the soil and sow the seed. They need to tend to the patch, waiting, watering and fertilising.

There is no immediate reward for the work a gardener does on any given day. They do not plant the seeds and eat the vegetables on the same day. It takes many weeks and months for the crops to grow and be ready for harvest. And yet the reward is great – there is something incredibly satisfying about picking fruit and vegetables from your own garden and eating them for dinner that night.

This feeling is similar, but so much better, when it comes to coaching your team. As a leader you'll feel a huge amount of satisfaction when you see the people you lead grow, develop and achieve new levels of performance as a result of your investment in them. And you'll reap the benefits over the long term as well.

Of course, coaching leaders don't just think about the long term benefits of coaching. They are also acutely aware of the long term impacts of failing to address underlying issues at the root cause. When leaders and their teams encounter problems in the workplace, so often the easy solution and the quick reward of resolving the surface problem doesn't deal with underlying issues. It simply kicks those issues down the road a little bit further.

Most people realise that the most valuable things in life take time to form. Diamonds are some of the most valuable substances on the planet. And most sources believe that it takes millions, if not billions, of years for diamonds to form. Similar timeframes are suggested for the formation of oil and many other of the world's most valuable substances.

Consider your most valued relationships. For the majority of people these relationships have lasted years if not decades and are valuable because of the trust that is being built and the experience is shared over that time.

For coaching leaders they believe their people are the most valuable asset in the organisation. And just as things of value in the natural world take time to form, so do the most valuable capabilities within the organisation – those of its people. Research shows that leaders who have developed long-term perspectives have better insights into the future.[1] They can better anticipate developments, opportunities and changes and are better equipped to guide their organisation through a modern, changeable landscape.[2]

It's important to look to your long term relationships – and coaching to develop those relationships – for the benefit of the individuals and your organisation as a whole.

Growth mindset vs fixed mindset

One of the most important things you can do as a leadership coach is adopt, and become a proponent of, the growth mindset. When a person wants to grow and develop themselves in any part of their lives, research shows they'll do far better, and accomplish far more, if they can adopt something called the 'growth mindset'.[3]

The idea of a 'growth mindset' (as opposed to a 'fixed mindset') was popularised by psychologist Carol Dweck in her book, *Mindset: The New Psychology of Success*.[4] The book shares her research – much of which was initially conducted in schools with children, but which has wider applications to anyone wanting to develop in any part of their lives.

So what did Dweck find during her years working with school children? Well, she found that there were two distinct mindsets. The first she described as a 'fixed mindset'.[5] A child with a fixed mindset believes that their level of intelligence, or skills and talents, are irrevocably fixed and there is really nothing they can do to change that. In other words, they either believe they are born smart or good at a particular thing. Or they believe that they weren't (and a fixed mindset can apply in both directions).

In contrast Dweck identified other students who demonstrated a different, more flexible, way of thinking. This was characterised by the recognition that while they might not be good at something *yet*, they could *develop* their level of intelligence about a subject, or their specific talents and abilities, with intentional effort and hard work. In other words, they could *get better with effort*. This mindset she labelled the 'growth mindset'.[6]

The difference between students (and people) who have a growth versus fixed mindset is sizable, and is easily shown in the way that an individual approaches a problem. Researchers have conducted brain scans on children who are working on a difficult problem.[7] While working on the problem all the children experienced some failures. Those children with a fixed mindset showed very little activity across areas of the brain associated with learning when viewing problems that elicited mistakes in their attempt to solve them.[8]

On the other hand, the scans of children with a growth mindset showed a flurry of activity as they sought to re-evaluate their answers and solve the problem in a different way.[9] Rather than giving up because they'd failed, these children saw their failures as stepping stones to eventual success.

> *In a growth mindset, challenges are exciting*
> *rather than threatening. So rather than*
> *thinking, oh, I'm going to reveal my weakness,*
> *you say, wow, here is a chance to grow.'*
> – Carol Dweck

We can simplistically view the fixed mindset as the ego mindset. For those with a fixed mindset, encountering challenges and difficulties is threatening. It risks exposing the limits of their intelligence or abilities. It risks exposing them as inadequate. A fixed mindset's response to failure is, 'I'm not good enough'.

Growth mindset is a vulnerable, open mindset. Those with a growth mindset see problems as an exciting challenge to overcome. They see it as an opportunity to learn, to grow and to get better. And because they aren't limited by their own fear of being exposed as 'not good enough' they lean into problems rather than running from them.

As a result those who possess a growth mindset are much more likely to set ambitious goals and work harder to achieve them despite any challenges that doing so might present. That's because they believe these challenges will make the outcome better (and they will).

Growth mindset in the workplace

Dweck's research in schools translates beautifully into the corporate workplace and has been widely applied in that environment. In fact, when I Googled 'growth mindset workplace' I got more than 13 million results – an incredible outcome. And this mindset has proved to be important on both the individual and company level.

Individual growth mindset in the workplace

Individuals who have a growth mindset are better able to focus on their own personal professional development.They embrace opportunities to learn new skills and gain new abilities in order to increase their individual performance.

Even better, individuals who possess a growth mindset have a greater sense of self-efficacy – the belief that they can influence the world around them. So, for example, when they encounter conflict, they're more likely to take responsibility for improving the relationship, brainstorm ways to make things better and identify ways to improve the experience across the entire workplace. A person with a fixed mindset in a similar situation is more likely to resign themselves to the status quo believing 'it is what it is and I can't change it'.

Company growth mindset in the workplace

Growth mindset is also important at an organisation level. Research shows that in organisations where a growth mindset is more predominant across the board, 47% of employees are more likely to see their colleagues as trustworthy, 34% are more likely to demonstrate strong ownership and commitment towards the company, 65% are more likely to suggest that the company supports risk taking and 49% are more likely to perceive the company as innovative.[10]

Growth mindset and coaching leaders

Coaching is all about the growth and development of people. And, as we've seen, for people to develop well, they need a growth mindset. So it's important that a coaching leader adopts a growth mindset. In fact, a growth mindset lays the foundation for a coaching mindset. And as Warren Bennis and Bert Nanus write, 'It's the capacity to develop and improve their skills that distinguishes leaders from followers.'[11]

For a coaching leader the growth mindset is vital. Without it there is no belief that the coaching approach will make any difference to outcomes or performance. Truly, any attempt to use coaching skills *without* a growth mindset is likely to come across as inauthentic and achieve lacklustre results (at best).

A leader without a growth mindset will look at their team and simply shrug their shoulders thinking that their team's current abilities and level of performance is all they will ever be capable of achieving. That thinking leaves little room or motivation for any type of coaching (which they believe will ultimately fail).

A coaching leader *with* a growth mindset, however, looks at the team and sees what they *could be*. They understand that with enough intentionality, effort and hard work achieving high performance is possible.

For these leaders, it's like looking at a large piece of raw marble. The first (fixed mindset) will see only a rock that cannot change. Others will look at that same rock and see the potential for a masterpiece. I'm sure this was the case as Michelangelo began to carve what would become the world famous statue of David. Michelangelo himself said, 'If people knew how hard I had to work to gain my mastery, it would not seem so wonderful at all'.

Fostering a growth mindset in others

Coaching leaders not only have to believe that getting better is possible for their own development as leaders – they also must believe the same is true of others. Further, they must believe that they can influence their people – that they can facilitate that growth and development.

There are many ways to foster a growth mindset in others (not least of which is the coaching process itself). These include:

1. **Teaching the growth mindset concept and encouraging its adoption**

   People can't be intentional about adopting a particular mindset or way of thinking if they can't first clearly articulate what that mindset is. Teaching the concept of a growth mindset, encouraging your team to use it and creating a positive environment that increases their chances to adopt it, is an excellent way to foster its implementation.

2. **Role model the use of growth mindset**

   It's important for you (as the leader) to walk the walk, not just talk to talk. So, if you want your people to adopt a growth mindset, you need to demonstrate the same style of thinking and approach. Don't be afraid to share with your team the areas that you are working on developing. Talk to them about how you are seeking to grow in those areas (or better yet, show them) and when appropriate even share your frustrations and struggles while doing so.

   When your team can see you striving to grow and develop, leaning into challenges and working hard to become better, they are much more likely to replicate your approach and do the same.

3. **Praise and reward the process**

   The growth mindset is much more about the process rather than the results. Of course both are still important and big wins should be celebrated. But it's just as important (or even more so) to celebrate your team's positive growth behaviours as they move along the process. Hard work and effort in their own growth learning and developing their ability to perform should be rewarded even if the desired results aren't achieved. After all, it's the hard work and effort that will produce results over time. And the failure to acknowledge praise and reward such efforts could potentially undermine a growth mindset and all the successes that it could ultimately bring.

Reflection time

1. Where do you sit? If you were to rate your current mindset between 0 (being 100% fixed) and 10 (being 100% growth), how would you rate yourself?

2. Where would you like to be?

3. What could you do to bridge the difference?

4. How would you rate the mindset of your team?

5. What could you do to foster a growth mindset across the team?

Key beliefs

While a growth mindset is the foundation of a coaching leader (and the foundation of a coaching leader's coaching), there are other key beliefs that inform their approach to both life and leadership. There are some common core beliefs that are often shared by leaders that adopt a coaching approach.

In this section I'll cover three:

1. People matter
2. People have the ability to overcome themselves
3. An empowered workforce is a good thing

People matter

An important part of a coaching leader's mindset is the belief that people matter and that investing in people is worth it. I recently worked with an organisation while they were going through a senior leadership transition. The first leader had been incredibly people oriented. He possessed a very relational and consultative leadership style and people considerations were always front and centre in his decision-making.

However, when this leader left the organisation he was replaced by a very different individual. This new leader was an engineer by trade. He very quickly made a number of structural changes to the organisation. And his approach was clearly towards the engineering organisational system that produced results rather than one that was set to lead teams of people to do the same.

Ultimately, however, this process failed. Because while an organisation can have the best strategy and systems in place, if there is no investment in people, it won't succeed over time.

Imagine you've invested in the design of a machine but failed to invest in quality parts or ensure that you're performing all the necessary maintenance. Ultimately, the machine will fail in the end. Because no matter how intricate and beautiful the design may be, when parts break or become worn the machine stops working.

People are the parts of the organisational machine. Without investment in the people the organisational machine either underperforms or eventually stops working altogether. Research backs up this theory as well.[12] In fact, findings show that factors of human capital investment – training, knowledge and skills – have a significant impact on an organisation's performance. And the higher the investment in training, the more the organisation's performance is enhanced. (Interestingly, the 'education' of employees didn't have any impact on performance.)

Robert Greenleaf, one of the seminal authors on the concept of servant leadership, points out that it's easy to lead perfect people, if only there were perfect people to lead.[13] So, since we don't have access to perfect people, we need to continually invest in the development and growth of our people, as well as in our own abilities to lead.

Good leaders know that investing in the human capital will pay dividends by unlocking extra discretionary effort that results in greater performance than you can even anticipate. As the capabilities of each member of your team increases, it's like replacing a regular piece of your machine with a higher quality version. Over time, the performance of that machine will be greater than even its original design.

People have the ability to overcome themselves

Everyone has the ability and the resources to solve their own problems and overcome their own challenges. Sometimes they just need some help to unlock and adopt a different perspective. And a coaching leader helps to do just that.

So often when people encounter problems they get locked onto those problems. In fact, they are so focused on the problems in front of them that they are simply unable to see any potential solutions. They lose awareness of what resources are available to them and forget to utilise past experiences that could inform future solutions. This often causes people to become frustrated, so they stop where they are and look for somebody else who can come in and solve the problem rather than find solutions for themselves.

But, if they were able to unlock their problem, take a step back and view the problem from within the broader context of their work *and* life, this higher-level perspective could reveal the actions they might take to overcome the challenges they face. They would be able to see the solutions for themselves and be able to remedy the problems.

Often people know what they need to do to remedy a problem. They might see that they're struggling with a lack of knowledge – and they can identify where to find that information. Or the problem might be capacity – and they are able to see how they might delegate tasks to people who are able to help. But often it's a case of people knowing what they could or should do and yet still not taking the necessary action.

I experienced this myself while writing this book. As I began I became so focused on writing the book I prioritised it over other activities that contributed to my wellbeing. There were no significant effects immediately but several months into the process I found I was having trouble sleeping, struggling to concentrate and easily losing focus. And I was becoming more easily discouraged, more easily frustrated at my kids and was struggling to maintain motivation.

I knew intellectually the source of my problems was a lack of exercise and healthy routines. Yet I had become so focused on the process of writing, I was failing to do what I knew I should. I *knew* what to do, but I couldn't take the right *action*. It wasn't until I engaged an executive coach myself that I was able to detach myself from the situation and could implement those healthy practices.

As my long-time mentor and good friend Dr Mike Allan often says – people are more brilliant than they know... but they sometimes need a little bit of help to realise it. That statement really captures the essence of the core belief that the coaching leader can unlock brilliance and harness the potential and innate ability to overcome. That was my personal experience. And it's been my experience working with coaching leaders as well.

The pygmalion effect

There is a theory in psychology known as the pygmalion effect.[14] This theory explores the idea that the way one person treats another can transform how that person sees themselves.[15] So our beliefs, perceptions and expectations of the people we lead influence their own self-perception and behaviours and, therefore, their performance. In short, people do better when we expect them to.

Once our people understand that we perceive them as capable of solving their own problems and expect them to do so, it increases the likelihood that they'll also believe that they can. This understanding can put them on the journey of seeking to meet new expectations. And this creates a self-fulfilling prophecy that results in increased performance.

The pygmalion effect was first brought to prominence by Robert Rosenthal and Lenore Jacobson in the book, *Pygmalion in the Classroom: Teacher Expectation and Pupils' Intellectual Development*, which outlined their research in a Californian school study.[16]

In this study students were given a disguised test of intelligence. A random selection of students was assigned to a random group of teachers for a year of tuition. The teachers were told that these students were specifically chosen because they showed promising results on the intelligence test. The hypothesis was that with this knowledge teachers would have greater expectations of their students and, therefore, treat them differently. At the end of the year those students showed significantly higher grades then the rest of their cohort despite the fact they were randomly chosen with no systematic selection based on intelligence.[17]

Of course, the pygmalion effect doesn't just apply to students in schools. It's also been shown to be prevalent within the workplace. A meta analysis reviewing 13 different studies shows that leaders' beliefs and expectations have a significant effect on their staff's performance.[18] Where leaders demonstrate greater expectation, staff have more engagement in learning activities and increased learning outcomes.[19]

The belief that people have the ability to overcome their own challenges and solve their own problems is central to the mindset of a coaching leader. Ara Parseghian, an American football player and coach who guided the University of Notre Dame to national championships in 1966 and 1973, once said, 'A good coach will make his players see what they can be rather than what they are.'

An empowered workforce is a good thing

There are leaders who like control. They are motivated by status and power. And leadership for them is all about satisfying their ego. These kinds of leaders give lip service to the concept of empowering their workforce and developing their people. But in reality they derive their sense of value from ensuring their team and organisation are reliant on them in order to achieve outcomes. This kind of thinking is the opposite of a coaching leader's mindset.

A coaching leader embraces an empowered workforce. An empowered workforce is one where staff are given the ability and opportunity to make decisions. They are allowed to use their skills and abilities to plan and deliver projects and initiatives without continual direction and micromanagement of their leader. An empowered workforce is one that has a significant contribution in determining what work gets done, when it gets done and how it gets done. Ultimately, an empowered workforce is the end game for all coaching.

In the military a force is always made up of numerous tactical teams that are often spread out across the battlefield. Each team and its leader will be briefed on its mission and know the battle plan. However as Prussian military commander Helmuth von Moltke famously said, 'No battle plan survives contact with the enemy.'

In battle the enemy often does unexpected things and circumstances change so quickly that tactical leaders don't have time to relay circumstances back to the force commander and wait for fresh orders telling them what to do. The doctrine of decentralised command dictates that tactical leaders are allowed to make decisions quickly on the ground that enable their teams to both survive and achieve the mission.

In many ways the dynamic and fast paced world that we live in today is much like a battlefield. The pace of change is constant and competitors are continuously doing the unexpected and disrupting the market. The amount of information that needs to be analysed and the speed of delivery required is greater than ever before. In many industries the only way companies can maintain a competitive advantage is by developing their staff and empowering their workforce. This decentralises decision making, speeding up the process, which allows organisations to remain agile. It is also the only way to fully leverage the benefits new technologies bring.

Three elements of an empowered workforce

Developing an empowered workforce requires three things.

1. **Organisational clarity**

   The first is organisational clarity. The workforce needs to fully understand the mission, strategy, goals and objectives of the organisation. Teams need to be clear not only on what they do, but why they do it. Only when this is a reality will the decisions team leaders make and the plans they develop be aligned with the direction of the organisation.

2. **Technical competence**

   The second thing required for an empowered workforce is technical competence. This requires teams and individuals to understand both their role in their industry and what good decision-making looks like within their organisation. Without technical competence any good decisions team leaders make are likely to be due to luck rather than a result of reliable capability.

3. **Secure sense of leadership identity**

   The final thing an empowered workforce requires is for the leaders to have a secure sense of identity. If a leader gains value and security from being in control or their team being reliant on them, then an empowered workforce will be perceived as a threat to their identity as a leader. A leader who gains a sense of value by developing and empowering others to operate without them, believes an empowered workforce is a good thing and will seek to create one in every chance they get.

Andrew Carnegie once said, 'It marks a big step in your development when you come to realize that other people can help you do a better job than you could do alone.' That realisation is the necessary catalyst for a leader to start passionately developing people at work.

Once the leader has experienced this realisation then they can begin experiencing the benefits that flow from empowering their own team. These benefits include spreading the workload and reducing their own stress levels and those of other high-performing individuals within their team. These teams will also be more proactive, demonstrate more initiative and operate more independently.

Empowering these teams and their managers to make decisions increases the speed and agility of performance which is great for the organisation. But it's also great for the individuals working in such environments. They will find their work more meaningful and feel like they are making a more valuable contribution to the organisation. And this will ultimately increase their own intrinsic motivation.

Benefits to the organisation

An empowered workforce provides so much benefit to an organisation. In fact, research shows that empowered workers have more depth of ideas, more opportunities to provide input and greater growth of both interpersonal and guidance skills[20] – which brings advantages to both the individual and the organisation as a whole.

Understanding the benefits that an empowered workforce brings to the organisation, however, is a central part of a coaching leader's mindset. It informs their intention to use coaching skills in order to enhance organisational clarity and develop technical competence so that they can decentralise decision making and empower their teams.

Me first, then others

An important part of the coaching leader's mindset is the belief that they need to apply coaching in their own life and in their own work before they can expect to coach others. If the leader's ultimate aim when coaching their people is to not just develop them but also to foster their own capacity to self-coach, the leader must first recognise the value of self-coaching. And that means engaging in it themselves.

The coaching leader must be intentional about developing their own ability to use coaching skills, both with others and in their own work, as well as being intentional about using coaching processes to solve problems, be proactive and demonstrate initiative. Eventually the use of these skills becomes so natural that they are infused into the way that they think and operate and lead.

An important foundational principle that applies to every leader, is that a leader should never be willing to ask others to do something they themselves aren't willing to. It speaks to the notion of the leader's integrity and credibility. As John Maxwell writes, '[C]redibility is a leader's currency. With it, leaders are solvent. Without it, they're bankrupt.'

For leaders seeking to introduce new behaviours or influence culture, the simplest process is to demonstrate the behaviour, teach it explicitly and then reinforce it over time. Leaders can't teach or reinforce behaviour with credibility if they haven't first demonstrated it. It's a bit like trying to provide financial advice when you're bankrupt. Or perhaps trying to provide nutritional advice when you're morbidly obese. Is anyone likely to listen? The same is true of leaders trying to encourage their people to coach and be coached.

Leaders need to lead by example, not only coaching themselves but also intentionally demonstrating coaching behaviours in conversations, during meetings, while managing projects and in the day-to-day leadership of their people. That includes being open to 'coaching up' from below.

Become comfortable with role modelling coaching behaviours

Many leaders haven't thought of themselves as role models for their people. And yet this is an important part of leadership. Being seen as a role model is something that effective leaders need to become comfortable with.

In my own masters research, I investigated the kinds of leaders that were more likely to be seen as role models by the people they led. What I found was that leaders who engage in behaviours intended to inspire and develop their people (such as coaching) were significantly more likely to be chosen as role models within their organisation. In many ways, coaching leads to leadership.

On the other hand, trying to teach coaching skills and encourage people to engage in coaching without role modelling a coaching mindset and coaching behaviours will only undermine your credibility and authenticity. Rather than building up trust and authority, you'll be doing the opposite, decreasing your ability to influence and, ultimately, eroding your overall leadership.

John Zenger and Joseph Folkman in their book *The Extraordinary Leader* write, 'Leaders are only willing to be as effective as those who in turn lead them.'[21] When it comes to coaching, your team will only ever become effective at using coaching skills to the degree that you, the leader, become effective at using those same skills.

One of the greatest ways for a leader to demonstrate the value of a particular concept is to embody the change that concept brings in their own world. Becoming effective at the use of coaching skills and applying coaching processes in your own work and leadership will allow people to see the change in you and experience the benefits.

People will watch what you do more than they will listen to what you say. They may echo what they hear but they will replicate what they see. Become the role model you want your team to replicate. Allow coaching to transform your world and inspire them to undertake their own transformation.

Reflection time

1. Which of these key elements of a coaching leader's mindset do you need to foster?

2. What would fostering these key elements change for you?

3. What is one thing you could do to foster such a mindset?

CHAPTER SIX

Skill set

'Once you have learned to ask questions – relevant and appropriate and substantial questions – you have learned how to learn and no one can keep you from learning whatever you want or need to know.'
– Prof. Neil Postman

When I was a boy, I loved Lego. Let's be real... I still love Lego. There is something about the colourful bricks and building of masterpieces that captivates my attention to this day. You can follow the instructions or construct your own creations. And your ability to create was limited only by your imagination. Once you had an idea, you just needed to choose the right Lego bricks and pieces to bring that idea to life.

It can be useful to think of a coaching leader's skill set as a box of Lego. Each skill is like a different Lego piece that can be selected and used or not, featured or hidden, depending on what the leader is trying to achieve in a given situation. While every Lego creation is made up of many selected Lego pieces, each outcome the leader achieves, the influence they exercise and the growth they enable is the result of the application of a selection of coaching skills.

There are many coaching skills and techniques that exist, almost as many as there are different Lego pieces. Don't worry I haven't listed them all. However I have dedicated the next three chapters to the coaching leader's skill set. Let's dive in and explore the 'how to' of coaching and the specific skills you can use to enhance your leadership and develop your people.

Listening

Listening is one of the first skills that a leader needs because it's listening that lays the foundation of leadership. And while listening may be one of the most basic skills in communication it is also one of the hardest to do well.

Studies show that people tend to inflate their own ability to communicate. In one study I recently read, 8,000 staff were all asked about the level of listening across their organisation. Almost every single one of them thought that they were better listeners than their colleagues.[1] But the reality is that the vast majority of us listen at only about 25% effectiveness rate.[2]

Listening lays the foundation for coaching.

This is an issue in the workplace. Ineffective listening increases the frequency of interpersonal conflict and the likelihood that conflicts will arise. But this isn't only a problem with staff. It's also a problem at all levels of leadership.

Another study done on LinkedIn recently surveyed 14,000 people across the world about leaders' soft skills, including the level of listening.[3] Of those 14,000 only 8% indicated that mid- to senior-level leaders in their organisation listened well.

As leaders we will struggle if we aren't able to listen well because it decreases our ability to understand those around us. When we aren't able to understand what our staff value and what drives them, we aren't able to motivate them either.

So really good listening – the ability to listen, and listen well – is actually a really rare thing, especially in leadership. But when we do it well, it is so valuable for people.

Listening drives self-belief

Carl Rogers, the famous psychologist, writes in his book, *A Way of Being*, 'We think, we listen, but very rarely do we listen with real understanding, true empathy. Yet listening, of this very special kind, is one of the most potent forces for change that I know.'[4] And the reason for this is that good listening, listening done properly, values the person that's being listened to. When we listen well to others, we are showing them that we consider what they think and what they say as important. We are showing them that they are *worth* listening to.

And when people understand that, when people have a sense that we value what they think and what they have to say, and that we value them as a person, that builds up their self-belief. And as we've previously spoken about, one of the key focuses of coaching is to build up that self-belief in people. It's this self-belief that allows them to make changes that are worthwhile, that can allow them to solve their own problems and eventually become great leaders themselves.

Listening establishes trust

Psychology teaches us that the therapeutic relationship (that is the relationship between the therapist and the client) is as powerful, or *more* powerful, than any particular treatment that the therapist might be using.[5] The relationship drives outcomes. But you can not have a healthy, supportive relationship – whether you're a therapist, a coach or a leader – if you don't have trust.

Listening establishes trust. And it's this trust that lays the groundwork for the relationship between the leader and the team. On the other hand, when staff come to have a discussion with their leader and they aren't listened to, it can be tremendously discouraging.

It's kind of like cooking a meal, cleaning the house and opening a nice bottle of wine all in preparation for someone to come for dinner... but they just don't show up. You've done the work, you've prepared and you're ready to share with another person, who simply isn't there. That level of disappointment and frustration is the feeling that our staff experience when we fail to show up in a conversation – when we fail to listen to them or actually engage with them. Disappointment. Discouragement. Frustration. Demotivation.

Part of the reason why listening is so hard is because the majority of people, they listen to respond rather than listen to understand. Most of us start out well, but after the first couple of words, we're already anticipating and thinking about what we are going to say in response. Because of that, we aren't actually *understanding* the speaker anymore.

As leaders we can't truly help our people if we don't understand them. And when we're working in a coaching capacity, we can't help them be aware of what's really going on if we aren't understanding what they are saying. We can't help them foster responsibility if we don't understand the person, what they need, what they're facing and what responsibility they need to take.

The art of listening

When it comes to listening, Shannon Alder, who's a therapist and an author, is quoted as saying, 'The most important thing in communication is hearing what is not said. The art of reading between the lines is a lifelong quest of the wise.' Simon Sinek echoes this sentiment when he describes the difference between hearing and listening. 'Hearing', he says, 'is listening to what is said'. Whereas, 'listening is hearing what isn't said'.[6]

So our role as coaches – as leaders who coach, to put it more precisely – is quite often to help our people unpack their thinking or identify what's going on underneath. And what that looks like in a practical sense, is listening to what they are saying and, importantly, identifying what's not being said.

This kind of listening is an active process. It takes intention and a conscious effort to do it well. And while much of this 'listening' is fairly basic, the difference between being exceptional at anything (including listening) and just being average is often the degree to which we execute the basics.

So, how do we do that when it comes to coaching as a leader?

1. **Eye contact.** Eye contact is important, but it also must be appropriate. Staring at someone or watching them too intently can make them uncomfortable. But if we're not making enough eye contact, people will feel like we're distracted or not engaged in the process. So make sure you have a good amount of eye contact, but with natural breaks.

2. **Body language.** Body language is also something that is really important to consider. Research undertaken by Albert

Mehrabian and Susan Ferris in the 1960s – and long held to be true – is that only 7% of our communication is actually done via the spoken word.[7] The other 93% is nonverbal – 38% based on how we use those words and the tone, speed, volume and pitch of our voice and 55% occurring through our body language.[8]

So making sure that we are intentional about our body language when we are engaging with our staff is really important. We want to be open and relaxed. We don't want to have crossed arms or crossed legs or slouch in the chair. And we don't want to be angled away from the individual that we're speaking to.

The best example of great body language, I believe, is Andrew Denton, the interviewer from *Enough Rope*. He is a master of body language when it comes to communication. You can see when he sits down that he's open, relaxed and ready to listen.

3. **Utilise encouragers.** Encouragers are those little things that we might say in order to show that we are engaged. These are the 'mm-hmms', 'uh-huhs', 'yeps', 'keep going' etc. These sorts of little words and phrases encourage the conversation to continue. They take minimal input from us, but show the speaker that we're still engaged in the conversation.

4. **Check for understanding.** Active listening means understanding, and that means checking ourselves. These are things like paraphrasing or summarising what's been said. And if we haven't quite got it right, and asking clarifying questions.

5. **Ask questions.** Questions bring the unsaid to the surface. They help you to read between the lines. When you explore

that you not only communicate better but you also help the speaker become aware of those things that they might be thinking or feeling that they aren't even aware of themselves.

Removing barriers to listening

Physical barriers create psychological barriers, and neither is good for a coaching leader. When you are coaching, try and remove all barriers between yourself and the person you're coaching. Research shows that while sitting behind a big (especially elevated) desk is one way to assert your power, it will have an inverse impact on your ability to communicate on a level with your staff[9].

In fact, it's so important to open, two-way communication that you'll never see a table or a desk in between a client and a psychologist in their office. In the same way, a leader who is coaching should not sit behind his desk. If there is a desk between you, it creates an incredible power differential, which can inhibit thoughts and ideas, and will negatively influence the relationship and rapport.

Once you've moved out from behind your desk, you then need to actively remove any other physical distractions. I remember when I was a young consultant I walked into the office of a CEO, who is now a vice president of a global company. At this point in time, she was CEO of an Australian company that had a global reach and did business with companies like IBM and the Australian Defence Force. So she held a pretty significant position. As I walked into the office, she turned and smiled and said, 'Hey Cliff'. Then she locked her computer, turned her monitor off, came out from behind her desk and gave me her full attention.

Now, you can imagine how that made me feel as a young consultant. She wasn't just giving me her attention. She was removing all the other possible physical disruptions. She was taking active steps to ensure that she wasn't disrupted. And it made me feel so valuable that she was willing to do that.

Actively taking steps to remove distractions demonstrates to our people that we believe they are worthy of our full, dedicated attention. And it's such a simple act to turn your phone on silent or turn your computer off.

But the reality is that listening, despite being one of the most basic skills of communication, is one of the hardest things to do. That's because it's not passive but requires intentional effort. We need to be conscious of our behaviors and our attention. But it's also important to be clear on the things to avoid.

What to avoid while listening

1. **Try not to identify the next question in your head.**
   Remember, most people listen to respond, not understand. In the coaching space, we often feel that it's reliant on us to have all these great questions and once one is dealt with, we feel pressure to be prepared to move immediately onto the next. So as the person we're coaching is talking and answering their questions, the temptation is for us to start to work out what the next question is, rather than really listening well.

   As you know, for me, when I learned to coach, this was the hardest thing that I had to overcome. I'd ask a coachee a question, and after the first three or four words of their answer, I was already starting to predict where their answer was going. And I would be thinking, 'Oh, that'd be a great question'. Or, 'I could ask this'. Or, 'I've been wanting to try that particular coaching technique and that series of questions. This will be a great opportunity to do that'.

My motivation was good – I wanted to improve my coaching and the outcomes for my staff – but by focusing on my own questioning, rather than really listening, I was no longer paying attention to what the other person was saying. And I became so focused on trying to figure out what my next question was that I was actually missing some of the most vital information that my coachee was giving me.

I've obviously improved this aspect of my coaching immensely. But it's still something that requires conscious effort for me. I have to quiet down my own inner voice and give my full attention to listening and to trying to understand what the other person is saying, and, importantly, about what is not being said.

2. **Don't take too many notes.** One of the other aspects of listening can involve taking notes and writing things down. This can be really useful when you want to check back for understanding. In fact, I'll often write down specific phrases or things that the coachee has said so that I can reflect their language back to them and clarify what they have said.

   However, you don't want to take too many notes. You don't want to spend the whole time writing things down because otherwise the individual may feel like it's an interrogation, or like you're gathering evidence. And then they may even feel that the 'evidence' might potentially be used against them at some point in the future.

   One of the tricks that I have used in the past when something really significant comes up is to ask a clarifying question around a particular insight or issue. Then I'll encourage the leader I'm coaching to actually write that down. So again, it's a balance of using note-taking and writing things down as an active part of engaging in the process, but not letting it overtake the process, not letting it impede the thinking and the communication that is occurring.

When it comes to listening, it's one of the things that we think we often believe that we do well, but in reality, we often don't. And this is what led Carl Rogers to write, 'We think we listen, but very rarely do we listen with real understanding, true empathy. Yet listening, of this very special kind, is one of the most potent forces for change that I know'. And that is the reality – that listening lays the foundation, not just for the dynamics in the relationship, but the foundation for powerful change.

Questioning

When it comes to coaching, questioning is a big part of the process. As a coach I use questions as a way to get to the bottom of what the leader needs, wants or is trying to achieve. But to do that, we have to be able to ask good questions.

So what constitutes a good question? I'm going to answer that question with one of the most annoying answers I could give. It depends. In reality, when it comes to what is a good question in coaching, context is everything. It depends on the topic, the relationship and rapport between coach and coachee, the stage of the coaching conversation and many other things. What might be an excellent question for one person, may not get any results with another. Or the same question might elicit two different responses with the same individual depending on when you ask it.

Before you begin to think that this is simply too hard and time consuming, there are some key principles that can help you ask good questions that can generally achieve the outcome you're after in almost any circumstance. Over time you will pick up and learn variations of these questions and when might be the best time to use them.

At the end of the day, all questions encourage our people to think. Our aim as coaching leaders is to ask enough questions that our people begin to ask themselves those questions and, in so doing, begin to think more for themselves. So I encourage you, trust the process.

Open vs closed questions

Coaching is a process that is built around dialogue. At its core, it's a conversation where one party is asking strategic questions to raise the awareness, responsibility and self-belief of another. In order for this process to work the conversation needs to flow. And the leader who is coaching needs to be able to ask questions that will facilitate the conversation and keep it going, keep it flowing. Thus in coaching, the general principle is that we prefer open questions rather than closed.

So what is the difference?

Closed questions are those that can be answered with a yes, no or one word answer. Take a look at the following example:

> Leader: Do you think this strategy will work?
>
> Coachee: No.
>
> Leader: Do you think if we had additional resources it might be possible?
>
> Coachee: Maybe.
>
> (Leader: Are you a difficult employee with a fixed mindset and negative attitude?
>
> Answer: Yes!)

As you can see, the conversation isn't going anywhere. It's not flowing at all. Even in cases where a leader is dealing with employees who have a positive attitude, closed questions don't promote good conversation. In this case, the leader is doing all the work to keep the conversation going. Ideally in a coaching conversation, the person being coached should be doing all the work – the majority of the thinking and the vast majority of the talking.

Open questions on the other hand, cannot be answered with single word answers. They require much longer answers and because of that help the conversation to keep flowing and moving. Let's take a look at the following questions:

- What do you think are the chances of this strategy succeeding?

- How do you think things will play out if we pursue this strategy?

- Where do you think we would end up if we sought to implement this strategy?

- What would it take to make this strategy work?

- When would be the right time to pursue this strategy?

How would you answer any of these questions? While it is possible to answer them with one word or very short answers, you have to work hard to do so. The chances are you are likely to answer these questions with much more detail. And that's why these open-ended questions facilitate the conversation rather than stall it.

When I was in primary school, I remember learning about the five Ws and an H. These are who, what, when, where, why and how. I was taught that the key to understanding a particular topic was asking questions with one of these words. In coaching, a leader is trying to facilitate understanding, both for themselves and their coachee. Therefore, good open coaching questions will usually start with one of the following: who, what, when, where or how.

Avoid using why

You will notice that I left 'why' out in the last sentence. Why is 'why' left out? Why is an interesting word which invokes a particular reaction from the human psyche.

When I'm teaching the art of questioning in my workshops, I will often ask someone to tell me a goal or aspiration they have. Once they share this with me, I will ask them straight back, 'Why do you want to do that?' The reaction is invariably the same. Muscles around the eyes and jaw tighten, eyebrows rise slightly. Often they will break eye contact and begin to shift in their chair. Sometimes they even turn their body away from me as they quickly try to come up with an answer. It is clear they are uncomfortable.

When faced with a question beginning with why, people automatically feel like they need to justify themselves. When we reveal why we do what we do, or why we want a particular outcome, we are revealing our internal thoughts, desires and motivations. This is a deeper part of ourselves that requires a level of vulnerability that is often beyond where we feel comfortable, particularly in workplace relationships.

As discussed earlier in the book, whenever we are vulnerable and share our inner thoughts and feelings, we take a risk. We risk being judged or criticised. The result is that people become defensive. The walls begin to go up and their psychological defences are activated as they try to retreat by turning the conversation to a more surface-level discussion that feels safe. Unfortunately surface-level conversations rarely result in insight, activate change, or facilitate personal growth.

Why questions make people feel like they are being interrogated. This activates the amygdala and the threat response system in our brains. This is the system responsible for the fight, flight or freeze response. Once activated, this system begins to take control and inhibits another important system in our brains that is crucial to successful coaching. That system is called the behavioural activation system.

The behavioural activation system is located in our prefrontal cortex, where our executive functioning, logic and reason take place. This system is what allows us to select behaviour that will be rewarded. It is the behavioural activation system that helps us project forward and evaluate which course of action we might take in order to get the results we desire. If coaching is all about helping people identify what they want and how to get it, the last thing we want to do is to inhibit this crucial cognitive system. And yet that is exactly what 'why' questions do.

Feeling threatened is the last thing a coaching leader wants their staff to experience when being coached. The intent is always to help the individual grow. However growth is unlikely when people feel threatened. What I encourage leaders to do when they are learning to coach is to avoid asking questions that start with why. We can elicit the same piece of information without using why. Simply by asking another open question starting with who, what, when, where or how.

Instead of asking *why* consider asking:

- What was the reason you made that decision?

- What was the thought process behind that course of action?

- How did you expect that to play out?

- Where did you think that choice would lead?

- Who did you expect to benefit from that?

With a little bit of intentionality, you can usually get the same information by asking one or two other questions, without making your coachee defensive.

Focus on the specific

Another strike against why-type questions is that, while why is very direct and to the point, it is also very generic. Asking why is asking for the broad brush reasons behind an issue. If you ask generic, broad brush questions, you will get generic, broad brush answers.

One of my mantras is, 'The more specific you are, the more meaningful you become.' This applies to the questions you ask. The more specific your questions, the more meaningful the answers you will elicit from your team. Often asking questions starting with who, what, when, where and how force you to be more specific and intentional with your questions.

Consider the questions beginning listed above. Instead of asking a generic why, they specifically target reasoning, thought processes, expectations and choices. The specificity of these questions is likely to result in more meaningful reflection and lead to greater insight for the coachee.

When to use why

You may be thinking you should be scrubbing why from your vocabulary completely. This is unrealistic and unnecessary. There is a place for why. However it is not as common as you might think.

Let's look at when you as a leader might get away with asking a why question.

1. When trust is high

In relationships where trust is extremely high and individuals are approaching the total rapport status we were talking about earlier in the book, individuals are much less likely to become defensive when asked why questions. In these relationships, the parties are familiar and comfortable with being vulnerable with each other having done so many times before. There is a track record of sharing inner thoughts and feelings without being judged and, therefore, individuals feel safe to do so again. The result is that when directly pushed to be vulnerable again by a why question, they feel comfortable doing so.

This is also the case in high-trust teams, where team members are used to being asked direct questions and having hard conversations. In these teams there are high levels of trust between individuals and high levels of commitment collectively focused on the team, its performance and its goals. Everyone understands that time is of the essence and having the hard conversations quickly with the purpose of moving things forward and holding each other accountable is part of each team member's responsibility. In these environments using why will not only be accepted but expected.

However, even in these high-trust scenarios, where asking why may not make people initially defensive, over using it still will. If you imagine that every relationship has a relational bank account where trust is the currency, then every interaction we have is either depositing trust into the account or making a withdrawal.

So, each time you ask a why question, it's like making a withdrawal from the trust account. It doesn't cause too many dramas if your account is full. However, too many withdrawals will start to cause problems. In the same way, too many 'why' questions will put a strain on any relationship.

2. When the issue is external

Many times when we are coaching members of our team, particularly around areas of personal development, the issues can be quite personal – whether it's around ways of thinking, choices they have made or behaviour they have displayed. That's not always the case though.

There are times when we might be coaching them around issues that are external to them. These might be around system and process improvements. It might be around other people. It might be around something that's happening in the market place outside the company. Because the issue is external to the individual and not personal, asking why doesn't automatically trigger the threat response.

That being said, it can be very easy for a why question to be interpreted as personal even when its intended target is an external issue. For example, a leader might be coaching one of their team around how they might improve a process they use within the company. The focus of the conversation is the process. It's external to the team member and should be an objective conversation. Yet consider the following two questions the leader might ask:

'Why is that the next step?'

versus

'Why do you do that next?'

Both questions are exploring the reason behind the next step in the process. But while the first one keeps the conversation external and objective, the second makes it personal. The second question has the potential, therefore, to trigger the threat response.

While it is possible to ask why questions in a safe way when coaching around external issues, it is very easy for a leader (particularly when they are learning to coach) to inadvertently make the conversation personal. Therefore I recommend leaders stick to asking who, what, where, when and how questions, even when tackling external issues.

The Five Whys technique

I'm often challenged by leaders who say, 'But what about the Five Whys? It's so effective'. I always agree with them. It can be very effective. But there is a specific way to use it when coaching.

The Five Whys technique[10] was developed by Sakichi Toyoda, a Japanese industrialist who made a significant contribution to the development of the 'lean' or 'just in time' philosophy[11]. Made popular by books like *The Toyota Way*[12], which made public its use across the Toyota organisation, this method is a form of root cause analysis. It seeks to uncover the root cause of a problem by repeatedly asking why. Usually by the time why is asked the fifth time, the root cause has been identified.

The following example is indicative of how this technique might be used with a software development team using Agile methodology.

> *Problem:* The client wasn't happy with the development team's performance and delivered negative feedback.
>
> *Why?*
>
> The team didn't deliver everything that was promised over the last sprint (two week work block).
>
> *Why?*

The workload was too high, the team over promised what they could complete in the sprint.

Why?

The team didn't factor in time for debugging code and addressing unexpected problems.

Why?

The team decision-making protocols weren't followed during sprint planning.

Why?

The team rushed sprint planning to get to the company social event.

This can be an extremely powerful tool for leaders to use and it definitely has its place. That place however, is rarely with an individual in a coaching or professional development context.

The best use of the Five Whys technique is in a group setting looking at collective or systemic problems. When a leader uses it with an individual, it is very easy for that individual to feel like they are being interrogated. Because they are. The Five Whys technique is designed to interrogate a problem. When that problem sits with a person, that person is then being interrogated. They will feel threatened, their amygdala will kick in, their defences will go up and your coaching will go out the window.

That being said, I have successfully used the Five Whys technique when coaching individuals. It does however take intentional framing to limit activation of the threat response system. In other words, you need to explain the method to the coachee, as well as how you're about to use it and the reason for its use. In this way they know what to expect and are mentally prepared for it.

In these situations, I might say something like the following:

> *So you have a real problem here and it doesn't seem like you really understand what's causing it. There's a technique called the Five Whys. It's a form of root cause analysis where we ask the question 'why?' over and over. Usually by about the fifth time we ask it, we have identified what the root cause of the problem might be. I'm wondering if it might be a helpful tool to help you identify what the cause of your problem might be. Would you be willing to give it a try?*

By framing it this way, being completely transparent with what you're doing and how you are using the technique, the individual being coached knows what you're doing and the reason you're doing it. They have agreed to participate in the process and expect the repeated why questions. In this way the coaching leader can neutralise the threat response as they tackle the problem head on.

While why can be used safely when we're intentional, it is very easy for leaders to misjudge its use and inadvertently make people defensive. So, it's still my recommendation that leaders who are learning to coach avoid asking questions starting with why.

Creating good questioning habits

There is another reason to avoid asking why questions when you're learning to coach and that's about forming good habits. Whenever we want to know the reason behind something, it's human nature to ask why. This seems to be part of our genetic blueprint as I'm sure any parent can attest.

From our earliest ages, one of the first (and most annoying!) questions children begin to ask is, 'why?' I'm convinced that Sakichi Toyoda didn't come up with the Five Whys technique – it was his children!

But because it's so built into our nature, learning to stop automatically asking why is hard. It takes intentionality and effort over time to retrain ourselves to ask different, richer and more specific questions.

After reading this you may start to notice how often you ask why questions. You will be mid conversation and kick yourself internally for asking another one. Even now, after coaching formally for over a decade, I will teach this principle in a workshop and pull myself up later in that workshop for asking a why question.

That's OK. You can't rewire the neural pathways in your brain overnight, when they have had a lifetime of reinforcement. Over time, by focusing on the better questions of what, when, where and how, it will become easier and more natural. These will start to become your default response to curiosity.

Scaling questions

Another type of question is called a scaling question. A scaling question is where the leader will ask the coachee to rate a particular item on a scale, usually from one to 10.

I love scaling questions because they are so versatile and so useful. I use them with all sorts of clients, in all sorts of scenarios and for all sorts of purposes. Here is an example of a typical scaling question I might use.

> *On a scale of one to 10, where one is absolutely terrible and 10 is awesome, how would you rate your ability to have difficult conversations?*

Asking a question like this causes the individual in front of you to stop and think in a different way. In order to answer it, they have to evaluate the situation so they can quantify it. This is not something that most people do naturally, so it requires a deeper level of thinking.

This can be especially effective for those who are thinking more emotively (right side of the brain) and might benefit from thinking more objectively or logically (left side of the brain).

The following are just a few ways you might use scaling questions when coaching members of your team:

- Identifying how difficult something might be

- Evaluating current skills and abilities

- Quantifying the effort required for a task

- Articulating the impact of a behaviour or situation

- Evaluating the quality of a piece of work

- Rating the priority of a particular item

- Quantifying confidence levels

- Identifying levels of commitment

Scaling questions can be useful in several different contexts:

1. Aid goal setting

Scaling questions help us to quantify aspects of the situation at a given point in time. It assists us to understand where we are currently, and provides a reference point for goal setting and determining where we want to be in the future.

Going back to our example around difficult conversations, if one of your leaders had rated their current ability to have difficult conversation as a six, you might then follow up with a question such as:

If you're a six now, where would you like to be in three months' time?

Note the use of the timeframe in this question. Remember, the more specific your questions, the more meaningful and targeted they become. This will encourage a greater level of focus from your team.

If your leader responds by indicating they want to be an eight, you can then ask what they need to do in order to get there. You may also break it down and ask what they need to do in order to move from six to seven and then from seven to eight. This approach easily allows people to identify what they need to do in order to move from where they are currently to where they want to be. Often they can easily articulate their own action plan as a result.

2. Measure progress

In addition to using scaling questions to set goals, they can also be useful to measure progress towards that goal. The rating given in response to a scaling question is able to be used as baseline data. Repeated use of the same questions can be used periodically to assess changes over time and measure progress – ultimately determining success and goal achievement.

3. Encourage deeper thinking and understanding

You can also use these versatile questions to explore issues in order to create a greater level of understanding for both you and your team. Following up a scaling question by asking your team member why they chose the rating they did is a great way to explore the issue at hand.

This will encourage them to think more deeply and critically about specific details of the situation. A handy tip when using this approach is to always ask why they didn't choose a number lower than their original rating, rather than higher. This is because asking them why they didn't choose a higher number will have them focussing on why they're not ready to get where they want to be or why they don't believe they can do it. It might even see them arguing against the change they're seeking! Asking them why they didn't choose a lower number makes them step up and argue *for* the change.

Of course the information elicited from scaling questions is self-reported data, subjective and likely to vary from person to person. But we're essentially asking individuals to quantify their own perceptions of the situation – and people's perceptions will vary. It's important to remember that the purpose of these questions is to encourage people to think differently and to facilitate progress.

People need to perceive a change in the situation in order for their perceptions of the situation to change. The conversation inspired by scaling questions is designed for individuals to identify what those desired changes might be and what they can do to make those changes. When it comes to scaling questions, progress is more important than accuracy.

Scaling questions are also a great tool for leaders to use in group settings with their teams, as you can simply calculate the average of all the team members' ratings to produce a collective rating. Additionally, comparing the different ratings between individuals within the team may provide useful insights for team leaders. Significant differences between the rating of individual team members may highlight the need for the leader to take steps to increase alignment amongst the team.

The miracle question

In line with Stephen R. Covey's 'Begin with the End in Mind' principle from his best-selling book The 7 Habits of Highly Effective People, the miracle question encourages the coachee to think about the desired end state they're hoping to achieve.[13]

Here's an example of a miracle question I might ask:

I want you to imagine that when you go to sleep tonight, a miracle occurs and your problem is completely solved. When you walk into work tomorrow morning, what will be different? How will you know the problem is solved?

I will usually follow this question up by asking the following:

- What will you see that is different?

- What will you hear people saying that is different?

- What will others be thinking and feeling that is different?

- What will you be thinking/feeling that is different?

By asking these follow-up questions, we're getting the coachee to articulate the detail in the outcome they want. The more clarity they have around the desired outcome, the easier it is for them to figure out a plan to achieve that outcome.

The miracle question is a creative way of asking 'What do you want?' It never ceases to amaze me how many people struggle to answer that simple question. From a psychological perspective, we know that human beings have a negativity bias.[14] We focus more quickly and often on the negative things in our world. While this in-built mechanism is designed to keep us safe by alerting us to threats, it means that often we focus on the problems we face and how to remove the problem, rather than thinking about what the most beneficial outcome would be moving forward.

While the two might not be mutually exclusive, they're rarely the same thing. When people describe the outcome they really want, they'll usually describe a situation where the problem doesn't exist. However, they never simply describe the current environment without the problem – it's always much more. They describe the benefits the solution to the problem brings.

The power of the miracle question is that it encourages individuals to think about benefits and outcomes, rather than problems. This means that as they start to identify potential solutions, they can focus on developing the options that will produce the desired benefits. As a result, the strategies or action plans people come up with are more likely to not only solve the problem, but do so in a way that also improves the workplace in other ways.

By articulating the desired outcomes and benefits of the solution, many people will be able to come up with a plan to achieve these. However, sometimes problems are particularly complex and it can be hard to find a way forward. The benefit of using the miracle question to paint a really specific picture of the end state, is that in these situations you have the opportunity to reverse-engineer potential solutions. You can choose multiple single details from the end state picture and figure out ways to achieve these. This results in a series of plans that attack the problem from multiple angles.

A classic example I've encountered multiple times is low team morale. It's a complex phenomenon and a problem no leader wants to face. Those who do will realise there's usually no easy solution – particularly when the root causes can be found in systemic issues within a large organisation.

In these situations, I'll use the miracle question to get leaders to paint a picture of the desired outcome and what high morale looks like. Amidst the broader description of what they would like to see, there are often specific details I take notice of.

They often say things like:

- The team would enjoy coming to work more.

- There would be more laughter and fun in the office.

- There would be more connection and people would eat lunch together rather than at their desks.

I then focus on one or two of those details. How could we make being in the office more fun? What would it take for there to be more laughter around the office? How can we encourage people to eat lunch together? How could we foster a greater sense of connection amongst the team?

Encouraging more laughter or fostering greater connection are much smaller, easier problems to solve than the complexity of poor morale. However, the combined impact of these will have a positive effect on the morale of the team.

Silence

I remember one of my most enlightening coaching sessions. I was coaching a leader who was responsible for an organisation with several hundred members. He was encountering a particular problem and was struggling to articulate exactly what the core of the problem was.

As I was coaching him, I was trying to be intentional about listening to understand, rather than listening to respond. As a result, when he finished answering a question I'd asked, I didn't have another question immediately lined up to ask him. I paused, giving myself a moment to think about what the next most valuable question might be given what he had just said.

The pause was probably only about four or five seconds, but that was enough of a gap for the leader to start speaking again. When he did, he made an insightful comment that revealed another element and perspective of the problem we were tackling.

Aware that progress was being made without any prompting from me, once he had finished speaking, again I remained quiet. I hoped the process might be repeated. He looked at me. I looked back. He broke eye contact as he continued to think about what he'd just said. After another 10 seconds of silence between us, he started to speak again. After only two or three words he stopped. 'Oh that's what the problem is!'

For the rest of the session he proceeded to outline what he needed to do to address the issue with very little input from me. He'd had a lightbulb moment that sparked a flash of clarity, which allowed him to see and articulate the way forward. And all I did was … nothing! I stayed silent.

Sometimes as leaders who coach, we can get caught in the trap of thinking that the quality of the coaching moment is totally reliant on us and the questions we ask. While there is some truth to this, we need to remember that coaching isn't about us. Coaching is always about the person we're coaching. Their development essentially comes from their own thinking, reflecting, exploring and articulating process. We can facilitate the process, but they need to do the hard work.

Great coaching outcomes don't result from first-rate coaching and questions from the leader and second-rate thinking by those being coached. Great coaching leadership comes from first-rate thinking from our people – even if it's prompted by the most basic coaching and questioning. Sometimes what's required for first-rate thinking is for us to stay silent and give our people the space to think.

What if the silence is uncomfortable?

People often find silence awkward and uncomfortable. And research shows us that there are strong reasons why.[15] First, silence can indicate non-compliance or confrontation (known as 'disaffiliative disfluencies'). And second, silence can be viewed as a social way of excluding others (the 'silent treatment').[16] On the other hand, 'conversational flow is associated with positive feelings of belonging, control, self-esteem, social validation, and perceived consensus'.[17]

To illustrate this point during workshops, I'll often stand at the front of a room and just stop speaking. After about three seconds, all eyes are focused on me. Then people start to avert their eyes, shuffle in their seats, fiddle with their pen, periodically looking back at me. They are uncomfortable.

It's all the same behaviour you'd expect to see if you were describing someone who was nervous. Some people start to smile and giggle, not knowing what else to do. Eventually, someone has to break the silence – whether it's with a question or a joke, the discomfort becomes strong enough that someone feels the need to fill the silence.

Using silence to your advantage

In a coaching scenario, leaders can use this discomfort to their advantage. When we remain silent, the individual we're coaching will feel the need to fill the silence – to keep the conversational flow going. By virtue of being in the middle of a coaching conversation, previous questions will already have this individual exercising their thinking muscle. Therefore, the need to fill the silence encourages them to think deeper about what's being discussed in order to elaborate on their last answer and have something meaningful to fill the silence with.

Often when we ask questions, we're encouraging our people to think laterally. We ask questions that encourage people to think in a different way or take a different perspective. This is often hugely beneficial and can provide profound moments of insight.

However, sometimes we don't need our people to think differently – we just need them to think deeper and to follow the same line of thought right through to the end, rather than stopping halfway. This allows them to discover the next step in the process, or to understand the second, third and fourth order effects of a particular course of action. In these moments, silence and simply providing space to think deeper is often more beneficial than additional questions.

The key to using silence as a coaching tactic

At the same time, we don't want to leave our people with the feeling of rejection. So, the key to using silence as a coaching tactic is to stay engaged. The person you're coaching needs to know you're fully engaged with them, even though you aren't saying anything.

During my undergraduate psychology studies, I spent time volunteering for Lifeline, the telephone crisis counselling service. I vividly remember a call one night where I overused silence. While I was intently engaged with the caller, she couldn't see that. The call ended with her yelling at me through the phone, believing I didn't care. I did care, but she couldn't see that. She thought I'd checked out of the conversation.

Communicating that you're engaged is much easier when you're face to face (whether in the room or virtually). Maintaining eye contact and demonstrating your focus is on the individual in front of you is key. The use of minimal encouragers can also be important. A simple 'mmhmm' or 'keep going' encourages people to continue thinking deeper without the complete silence becoming so awkward it detracts from the process.

This becomes more important in scenarios over the phone, where there are no visual cues. For example, I could and should have used more minimal encouragers on my Lifeline call to communicate my engagement with the caller.

Reframing

Another important coaching skill for leaders to learn is the ability to reframe conversations. Many of you will be familiar with the concept of 'above and below the line'. Where above the line is positive, characterised by qualities such as ownership, accountability and responsibility, and below the line is negative, demonstrated by blame, excuses, deference and denial.

The 'above and below the line' concept really captured a wide audience after being explained in the book *Walking the Talk* by organisational culture expert, Carolyn Taylor.[18] In that book, she mentions learning about the idea from her friend Robert Kiyosaki (author of *Rich Dad Poor Dad*[19]).

Today this concept is used in organisational programs by the largest consulting firms in the world (and many others). Implementing it involves helping teams elicit behavioural expectations – listing what behaviours they expect to be demonstrated by team members (above the line) and what behaviours they don't want to see (below the line). This is a great activity I often take teams through as it's another example of clearly articulating expectations so team members can be collectively intentional about how they behave.

The above and below the line analogy can also be used in the context of mindset. An above the line mindset is characterised by the qualities of ownership, accountability and responsibility. Blame, excuses and denial are evidence of below the line thinking. Ideally, we want our team to stay above the line and maintain a positive mindset. However, anyone who has been in leadership for more than five minutes has encountered the negative thinking of people below the line. Reframing is an important tool to shift that thinking.

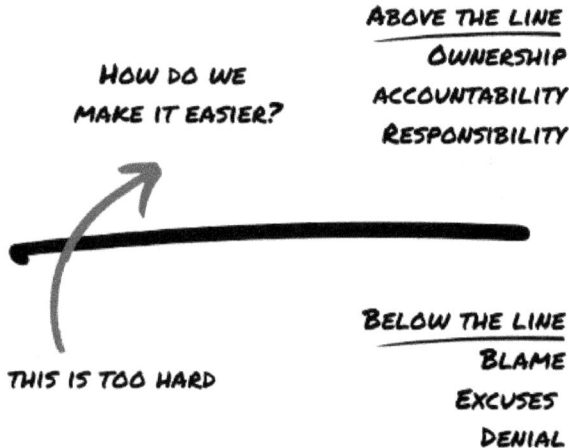

ABOVE THE LINE
OWNERSHIP
ACCOUNTABILITY
RESPONSIBILITY

HOW DO WE MAKE IT EASIER?

THIS IS TOO HARD

BELOW THE LINE
BLAME
EXCUSES
DENIAL

Reframing starts with the language people use. What people say provides us with an insight into their mindset and thinking. People who are trapped in a negative mindset will use negative language. They often say things like, 'This is too hard' or 'We can't do this' or 'That will never work'.

Simply telling people to stop having a negative attitude and to be positive rarely works. Instead, they just become defensive believing that the leader doesn't understand or support them. Leaders need to be able to challenge people's negative thinking and help them adopt and maintain a positive mindset, without triggering their defence mechanisms. That's where reframing comes in.

The technique of reframing

The technique of reframing is to take the phrase or sentence that indicates the negative thinking, identify the negative word, reverse it to make it positive, then frame the sentence in a question.

So for example, when reframing 'This is too hard', the negative word is *hard*. The reverse or opposite of hard is easy. So when you frame it in a question, it becomes, 'How do you make it easier?' When you encounter, 'We can't do this,' you might respond with, 'How could you do this?' When you hear, 'That will never work,' try countering with, 'What will make it work?'

Reframing works because it takes the conversation and the thinking from problem-focused to solution-focused. The technique involves asking a question. In order to answer that question, people have to think about the answer. If the question comes from a positive perspective and is solution focused, people need to think in a positive way to provide a solution-oriented answer. In this way, a leader can help facilitate a thinking and mindset shift from below the line to above the line.

There are always multiple ways to reframe a statement. If you are looking for inspiration, look to the five Ws and H. You can reframe any statement using who, what, where, when and how. Again, I recommend avoiding the fifth W, why, when reframing. Why gives people an opportunity to justify their negative mindset. Such justifications usually turn into an excuse. We want reframes to be open questions that require positive thinking and solution-oriented answers.

Have a look at the table below. Have a go at providing additional reframing questions for the statements in the left hand column.

Statement	Reframe	Additional Reframe
'I can't do this.'	How can you do this? Where could you do this? When would you be able to do this? Who could help you do this? What do you need to be able to do this?	*Where could you do this?* *When would you be able to do this?* *Who could help you do this?* *What do you need to be able to do this?*
'This is too hard.'	How can you make this easier?	
'This will never work.'	When will this work?	
'They don't understand.'	What do they need in order to understand?	
'We don't have the budget for this.'	How else could we fund this?	

One of the reasons why this technique is so powerful is that it starts with the language and thinking of the person in front of us. This is meeting the person where they are. It implicitly acknowledges the individual's experience and demonstrates a level of understanding from the leader. There is a subtle level of empathy and connection that occurs. This can be accentuated by explicitly acknowledging the experience immediately prior to asking the reframing question.

An example might be, 'I know this situation is really hard. How do you make it easier?' There is a temptation when doing this to use the word 'but' in between the acknowledgement and the reframe. Be careful not to do this. This invalidates the acknowledgement you've just made and therefore the experience of the leader in front of you. More on this later.

While reframing begins with a validation of a person's experience, it doesn't leave them there. It challenges them in a way that positions them to move them forward. Once people shift into an above the line mindset, they are more able to identify different options, articulate solutions and develop action plans in order to implement those solutions.

Reframing in teams

Reframing is also a highly versatile technique. It can be used in both one-on-one conversations and team environments, and can become a powerful tool for team accountability.

There was one team I worked with for whom the concept of reframing really resonated. They had all received coaching skills training and were familiar with the above and below the line concept and reframing as a technique. Whenever someone would make a negative comment around the office, the other members in the team would throw something at them and get in their face saying, 'That was below the line. We're not letting you go until you reframe that comment three different ways!'

It was all done with lots of laughter and everyone was on-board with it. They used reframing as a mechanism to keep each other accountable to maintaining a positive mindset around the office. As you can imagine, this team had a very healthy culture and it was a fun environment to work in.

Reframing ourselves

For leaders, the other important use of this tool is to reframe our own thoughts. Leadership is hard and often lonely as we carry the pressures and responsibility for the support, development and performance of our people, our teams and the organisation as a whole. Just as we need our people to be able to stay above the line, we need to be able to think positively and maintain a solution-focused mindset ourselves.

I remember speaking to a friend of mine one day. She'd had a pretty tough day. She identified that her own negative thinking in response to her work circumstances was part of the problem. I shared with her the concept and technique of reframing.

She went to work the next day and was intentional about continually reframing her own thoughts. She came home at the end of the day and reflected on how good the day had been. The next day she forgot to reframe and things didn't go so well. That evening she questioned why the day before had been so good and that day was so bad. She realised the difference has been her use of reframing. She was intentional about reframing for the rest of the week and when I saw her that weekend, she reported finishing the week on a really positive note.

Now, this was a really important skill for this individual, considering she was a paediatric oncology nurse. Being surrounded by kids with cancer each day was immensely challenging. If she was to care for them and help them stay positive, she had to stay positive herself. For us as leaders, learning to reframe our own thoughts is often more important than reframing other people's thinking.

Reframe here, reframe there

Reframing is a great technique for leaders to have in their back pockets. Once a leader has this technique in use, whenever they encounter negative thinking they can gently challenge that thinking in the moment. It might be in a meeting, during a one-on-one with a team member or casually over lunch with a peer from another department. As the leader goes about their day with a reframe here and a reframe there, they're continually lifting people's thinking, helping to find solutions and maintain a positive mindset across the organisation.

And people love it. Reframing makes people feel good. Thinking positively and identifying solutions in order to make progress feels good. If you are continually reframing and helping people do these things, they will walk away from your interactions feeling good about you and your leadership. That develops trust and leadership capital over time.

Things to avoid

Leading questions

A leading question is one that implicitly directs or prompts a person towards a particular predetermined answer. Generally, leading questions are a type of closed question that can be answered with either a yes, a no or a one word answer.

As previously mentioned, we already want to avoid closed questions in a coaching conversation, in order to keep the conversation flowing. However, there's another reason you want to avoid leading questions –

because they are generally at odds with what we are trying to achieve when we coach.

When we ask a leading question, we are implicitly directing our staff towards the answer we want. We become the ones who are doing the thinking and solving the problem. We are then simply communicating that solution using a question. We may as well be telling our staff what to do.

The whole purpose of coaching is to encourage our staff to think more deeply – to engage their brains in critical thinking and creativity in order to solve their own problems and find their own solutions. When we ask leading questions, we are doing the thinking for our staff and giving them the solutions. In doing this, we fail to foster self-belief in our staff and their ability to come up with valuable solutions. We fail to inspire ownership of those solutions, the process of their implementation and the ultimate outcome.

Asking leading questions is tempting for leaders who are learning to coach, because you get all the benefits of telling your staff what to do (it's quicker and you get the solution done the way you want it done) while feeling like you are coaching and empowering your staff. The reality is, however, in asking these types of questions you're maintaining your staff's reliance on you as a leader and not empowering themselves to think critically, creatively, independently and with initiative.

Using 'but'

Another word to avoid is the word 'but'. Removing 'but' from your vocabulary doesn't just apply to coaching, it will be good for your leadership in general. The word 'but' is a conjunction. It is used to connect two thoughts or sentences together. However, when we use the word 'but', we invalidate or devalue the thought that comes before it.

This is known as invalidation. And research shows that this can cause significant damage to a person's psychological health and wellbeing.[20] When someone feels invalidated, they believe that their emotional experiences and responses are insignificant, unreasonable or unacceptable.

Consider a leader making the following statement:

You've made some really great progress but you still haven't met this quarter's target.

The implicit message that this statement communicates is that the leader is not really interested in the great progress that's been made. They're only interested in whether or not the quarter's target has been met. Diminishing the value of the progress that's been made could be really deflating for team members who have put in significant effort to get this far.

Rather than using but, I encourage leaders to use 'and' instead. 'And' is another conjunction. While it performs the same linguistic function as 'but', it communicates a greater equality between the thoughts it connects. This simple swapping of words can have a significant impact on the message we communicate and the people we lead. Consider the following:

You've made some really great progress but at the same time you haven't met this quarter's target.

versus

You've made some really great progress and at the same time you haven't met this quarter's target.

Take a moment and think about the difference between the two statements. Do they feel different? Did you read the sentence with a different tone inside your head? The first statement feels like a rap over the knuckles, while the second is much more encouraging without diminishing the fact that a performance gap still needs to be addressed.

Here's another example:

> *I know you had positive intent but you really offended your colleague.*

> versus

> *I know you have positive intent and at the same time you still really offended your colleague.*

The first statement disregards the fact the individual had positive intent and was trying to do the right thing. The focus is solely on the offence that was caused. And this can cause those awful feelings of invalidation.

The second statement, however, balances the focus. It acknowledges the positive intent, while still acknowledging the need for better delivery and execution.

Avoiding the use of 'but' is another hard habit to break. However, with a few more 'ands' and a little more intention with the language we use, the payoff will be felt in the relationships, rapport and trust we build with those we lead.

Reflection Time

1. Which of these skills resonate with you the most?

2. Where, when and how will you start to use them?

CHAPTER SEVEN

Goal setting

No one ever accomplishes anything of consequence without a goal... Goal setting is the strongest human force for self-motivation.
– Paul Myer

Goal setting sits at the centre of coaching. It is an essential skill and there is so much to write on the topic that it gets its own chapter. Whether the focus of coaching is to achieve a certain result or solve a problem, the most effective starting point is always articulating the desired endstate and outcome you are working towards. In other words, the goal. As a coaching leader, the ability to effectively set goals is crucial for our own practice as leaders, as is our ability to coach others to do the same.

SMART(PP) goals

When it comes to developing goals, many people are familiar with the SMART goal formula which was introduced by George Doran in the November 1981 issue of *Management Review*.[1] As you can see, it's been around a long time. However, whenever I teach goal setting, I am constantly surprised how many people and leaders have not learned this method. I'm even more surprised at the number of leaders that have learned it, but don't use it in their work and lives in general.

SMART is an acronym for each of the considerations required for a clear, concise and actionable goal. Here's how it looks:

→ Specific

→ Measurable

→ Achievable

→ Realistic

→ Time-bound

To make SMART goals even more powerful, I like to add two further considerations.

→ Positive

→ Purpose

Let's take a closer look at each step.

Specific

The difference between an aspiration and a goal lies in specificity. Aspirations are general. Goals are specific. Consider the following statements:

1. I want to be a good leader.

2. I want to develop a high-performing team.

3. I want to be better at a particular task.

Let's explore these statements a little.

1. **'I want to be a good leader.'**

   What is a good leader? Most would say a good leader is someone that inspires trust in those they lead. If you have the complete trust of your team but they consistently fail to achieve results, are you a good leader?

2. **'I want to develop a high-performing team.'**

   If your sales team consistently makes budget early each quarter, are they a high-performing team? What if the team also has a toxic culture, is full of conflict and everyone wants to leave?

3. **'I want to be better at a particular task.'**

   Similarly, what does being better mean? If you want to be better at a particular task, does it mean doing it faster? If you increase the speed at which you complete the task, but make more mistakes, are you better at the task?

Hopefully you will see that the general nature of these statements indicates a lack of focus. If we don't know exactly what we want to achieve we can't work out what we need to do, or know when we have actually achieved our desired outcomes.

On the other hand, when we get specific and identify details, we bring clarity to what we want to achieve. And when we are clear about what we want to achieve, we are much more capable of working out what we need to do in order to achieve it.

So, for example, improving communication when delegating tasks and building trusting relationships with team members is much clearer than just wanting to be a 'better leader'.

Understanding what is required to foster a culture of psychological safety and implement effective peer-accountability systems is better than simply wanting to create a 'high-performing team'. And being able to produce a board paper in under three hours without having it sent back for corrections by the CEO has much greater clarity than either of the previous tasks. Being able to identify and focus on the actions required to make them happen is the best way to get the outcomes we want.

Measurable

Goals need to be measurable for two reasons. First (and primarily), we need to know whether or not we have achieved our goal. If we cannot measure our performance, how do we know when we have achieved it?

How specific our goal is, how much detail and which details we include will often determine how we measure success. Taking the 'I want to be a better leader' example above, if we simply say we want to build trusting relationships how do you know if you've achieved that goal? If, however, we make it a goal to see an increase in the trust scale on the next organisational engagement review, we can very clearly measure our success. Either the scale rating increases or it does not.

The second reason goals need to be measurable is that we need to be able to measure our progress so we can determine when new or different steps should be taken. If we are trying to gain 50 new clients by cold calling and after three months we have only made one new client, we may need to look at digital marketing or different forms of networking to meet our goal.

On the other hand, if our goals are not measurable, we will never know if our strategy for achieving them is working. If we can see no progress being made, we need to try something else. Otherwise, we become discouraged and give up. But when we do see progress we feel good at what we have achieved so far and become motivated to continue. As a result, the process of achieving our goals becomes more enjoyable and more satisfying.

Achievable

If our goals are not achievable, we will never accomplish what we set out to do. And if we set goals that are not achievable, this can cause us to question our own ability and become disenchanted with those areas or aspects of our lives.

As a young boy, all I ever wanted to do was become a fighter pilot, following in the footsteps of my grandfather who flew in WWII. But the reality is that I was born with imperfect vision. As a result I could never pass the medical assessment required to enter the Air Force as a pilot.

If I had held onto this dream and related goals, I was doomed to fail from the beginning. Likewise, if I wanted to be President of the United States of America, such a goal is impossible because I was not born in that country, so I'm prohibited from holding that office by the US Constitution.

If we repeatedly set unachievable goals and fail, we begin to question not only our ability, but our self-worth as well. The result is many people give up on achievement, personal growth and development of any sort, resigned to live an aimless life of mediocrity. I don't want you to be one of those poor souls. So if the goal is unachievable, why are you wasting your time and effort in trying to achieve it?

The achievability of goals

Two points to note about achievability of goals. First is that we need to be aware that often, what determines whether goals are achievable or not, lies outside of our sphere of influence. In the example above, I had no influence over the physical entry standards set by the Air Force. The decision was made by the broader 'system' which was against me. The same can be said of the requirements for presidential candidacy.

Be careful setting goals that rely too heavily on the actions/decisions of others to achieve the desired outcome. You can only control your own behaviour. You cannot control others. Where possible, set your goals where you are solely responsible for and in control of the outcome.

The second point to note is that just because something has never been achieved before, doesn't mean you cannot achieve it in the future. If the achievability of goals was limited to what has already been accomplished, innovation would be dead and the progression of both society and individuals would be non-existent.

'Whatever your mind can conceive and believe, it can achieve'.[2] You may just have to set and achieve some slightly more possible goals first, to achieve a platform from which to spring forth into the impossible.

Realistic

One of the biggest killers of goal achievement is unrealistic goals. People trying to achieve too much, too quickly often experience burnout and discouragement. Rather than reassess and adjust their goal to a more realistic target, they invariably give up.

If I was overweight and had never participated in an endurance sport, it would be unrealistic to set a goal to qualify for the Hawaiian Ironman. Is it conceivably achievable for someone with the right focus and training to do so? Yes. But is it likely that an ordinary person will make such a radical life-style transformation and make it to Kona? Probably not.

Making goals realistic should not disqualify your big dreams that require large amounts of achievement. But your goals should focus your actions on what you can realistically do to achieve your dreams.

For example, when Australian cyclist Anna Meares first arrived at the Australian Institute of Sport as a teenager and declared to her new coach her goal was Olympic gold, he told her it was unrealistic and unachievable for her.[3] At the time she walked away in tears, shattered. But together she and her coach focused first, on the world championships the following year.[4]

After she achieved success at the world championships, her coach sat her down saying, 'OK, Olympic gold is now on the table.' By the end of her career, with a total of six Olympic medals, two of which were gold, Anna is the most decorated female track cyclist in history. But had she kept her aim too high, too early, she may never have achieved what she did.[5]

Time-frame

In addition to the size of our goals, two other factors often determine whether goals are realistic or not. These are frequency and time-frame. One of the most common fitness related goals is to go to the gym or exercise every day or five times a week. For many people this is unrealistic. Most start off well enough, but by week three (if they last that long) they are too tired, or become too busy and stop. Those that aim for twice a week, then increase it to three times a week after a month or two are much more likely to continue.

Similarly, trying to increase trust levels, change team culture or make a million dollars in one month are all equally unrealistic for most leaders.

When setting realistic goals it is important to ask yourself, do I have enough time, and is it sustainable? If yes, then you need to move on to the next step and set a deadline.

Make sure goals are time-bound

It's all well and good to set a clear and concise goal that is measurable, achievable and realistic. But if you stop there, the question becomes when will you actually achieve it? If you don't set a timeframe and decide on a deadline, then you'll put it off to tomorrow. And tomorrow you'll put it off until the next day. As the old adage goes, tomorrow never comes.

However, when you put time limits on the achievement of your goal, you make it a priority. Think about it. Whether at school or at university, what happened the night before an exam? Everything else was set aside so you could study. Preparation for the exam became top priority.

The same principle applies to our goals. When we set timeframes and deadlines, we make achieving the goal a priority. This spurs us into action.

Timeframes should not be too short, or they'll make the goal unrealistic. But they shouldn't be too far into the distant future. When we allow too much time for the achievement of our goals, it doesn't require action right away and there's no impetus to start. We're liable to think, 'I have plenty of time. I'll start tomorrow.' So, we put off starting and usually forget about the goal, only to remember at a time too close to the deadline for the goal to be realistically achievable.

Another danger of extended timeframes is that the challenge of achievement is not great enough to keep our interest. If it's too easy, it just won't hold our attention. So, part of the art of goal setting is picking the right timeframe in which to achieve our goals.

Positive

Positive is the first 'P' that I add to the SMART Goal formula. This is talking about framing the goal in a positive way.

But what does this mean? Well what I mean is that we want the goal to be something we want to take positive action to move towards, not something we want to stop doing. What we can learn from psychology is that we move towards what we focus on.[6] When we are goal setting, the subject of the goal is what we are focusing on and what we will move towards. If our goal is to 'stop doing X', the subject of the goal, or what we are focussed on, is still X. Because we are focusing on X we are still likely to keep doing X.

Psychologists often use this principle when working with their clients who want to change their behaviour. For example, let's say your goal is to quit smoking and so you attempt to do so by constantly thinking, 'I'm not going to smoke, I'm not going to smoke,' every time you feel the urge. Where is the focus? On smoking. As a result, most people will continue to smoke.

On the other hand, if we reframe our goal to having clean and healthy lungs by establishing a healthy habit of eating fruit and drinking water, when the urge to smoke comes, our focus is now on establishing healthy habits. Because our focus is now on healthy habits and not on smoking, you are more likely to engage in those habits and less likely to smoke.

Remember we move towards what we focus on. When we set goals that are positively framed and focus on what we want to do and achieve (rather than what we want to stop doing) we are much more likely to be successful.

> *'If you want to be happy, set a goal*
> *that commands your thoughts, liberates*
> *your energy, and inspires your hopes.'*
> – Andrew Carnegie

Purpose

To take the process one step further and increase the importance we place on achieving our goals, we add the second 'P'. This 'P' is for purpose. And with it we are asking ourselves, what is the purpose of achieving this specific goal?

At this stage it's about being able to clearly articulate how this goal contributes to your personal vision. When you clarify *why* you want to achieve a goal and link it to your purpose in life, your values or a contribution to a cause bigger than yourself, you inherently increase its importance. It also helps to motivate you when you face obstacles or are struggling to maintain the consistency needed to achieve our goal.

'I will establish a healthy habit of eating fruit and drinking water by 30 June, so I can have clean and healthy lungs allowing me to be more active with my children,' is much more purposeful and motivating than just, 'I want to stop smoking.' Likewise a motivating goal for the coaching leader might be, 'I will invite feedback at each weekly meeting to help foster psychological safety so people feel able to raise issues and deal with conflict early.'

SMARTPP goals add an extra layer of motivation that steels our commitment and reinforces the importance of our success.

'Goals not tethered to your purpose are wild goose chases, and a purpose without [SMART-PP] goals is a fantasy awaiting regret.'
– Commander Mark Devine

Boosting goal achievement

There are several actions that leaders and their teams can take to increase their level of motivation towards achieving goals. The first is asking two simple questions:

1. How important is achieving this goal for me?

2. What am I willing to sacrifice?

How important is achieving this goal for me?

The best way to answer this question is to actually put a number to it. Ask yourself – on a scale of 1 to 10 (1 being not important and 10 being our top priority), how important is it? Let's say we score a goal seven out of 10 in importance. We can then ask ourselves, what is the difference between a seven and an eight? What could I do to make this goal more important to me?

My rule of thumb is that if we score a goal any less than a seven, it is not likely to be important enough for us to give it the priority it needs to be achieved. Therefore, if we are honest and score our goal a six, is this really a goal we should be investing our time and resources into achieving, or should we be pursuing more important things in life? If we decide that this goal is worthy of our investment, how do we get it from a six to at least a seven, if not higher?

What am I willing to sacrifice?

This is a great question because it helps us determine where this goal sits in our priorities. Most people live 'busy' lives, full of different activities that take up our time. As a result, for us to dedicate time towards achieving our goal, we have to take that time from somewhere else. To do what is required to achieve our goal, we need to stop doing, or do less of, something else. We must sacrifice something less important to us.

So what are you willing to sacrifice? Answering this question prioritises your goal amongst your other commitments, interests and habits. It clarifies how important the goal is to you.

Write it down and tell someone

Now that you've got your goal you need to take the next critical step – write it down and tell someone. This is a simple step. Yet it is powerful enough that it is worth a specific mention.

What is it about the simple act of writing? It brings clarity. Remember this quote? 'Thoughts untangle themselves over the lips and through the fingertips.' Writing forces us to articulate our thoughts. Articulation brings clarity. Clarity allows us to aim accurately. For anyone who has fired a rifle, you will know you cannot hit the target if you cannot clearly see it.

Gail Mathews from California's Dominican University has studied goal setting and goal achievement in detail. Her research found that goal achievement is significantly increased when we write our goals down.[7] However there were two other activities that further increased the likelihood of success. The first is sharing your goal and making a public commitment. The other is measuring and sharing progress reports to others.[8]

When we tell someone we are going to do something, they expect us to do it. So when we share our goal with others, there is an expectation we will take action towards it. The next time we see them, they're even likely to ask us how we are going with our goal. If we haven't taken action we fail to live up to their expectations (let alone our own). This leads to an uncomfortable conversation as we try and justify (to ourselves as much as to them) why we failed to meet their expectations.

At a deeper level, we fear disappointing others. Psychologically, fear is a powerful force behind much of our behaviour.[9] By sharing our goal we are leveraging that subconscious fear to motivate ourselves towards positive action.

Review your goals

One of the most common reasons people don't achieve their goals is that they forget about them. The busyness of life takes over and the *urgent* takes our attention away from the *important*. Even those who set SMARTPP goals are susceptible. Before we realise it, months have passed, we haven't taken action and it's now unrealistic for us to achieve what we had initially intended.

This is the single biggest reason I have not achieved goals in the past. Big achievements are the result of accumulated small achievements. These are produced by small actions taken regularly. If we do not remember to do the small things regularly, achievement requires large efforts less frequently. For most this is much harder.

So, how regularly should we be reviewing our goals? If the busyness of life and the urgent demandes intrude on a daily basis, then we should remind ourselves of our priorities – and therefore our goals – with the same frequency. In other words, daily.

Yes, it takes discipline to take the time to review your goals every single day. But remember, we invest our time in what we value. If we are committed to achieving our goals, we must remind ourselves of them every single day. Or we risk losing them in the other demands of our lives.

Measure progress

Measuring your progress towards a goal has multiple benefits.

1. First, it tells you whether you are pursuing the right strategy. I spoke about this earlier when I outlined why goals need to be measurable.

2. Second, it keeps you motivated.

Progress is the small achievements that accumulate to create big achievements. When we see progress, we have achieved something. This success releases a hit of dopamine in our brains which makes us feel good. Our belief in our own ability is reinforced. Our self-esteem increases. We experience positive emotions. As a result, we want more of what feels good. Our motivation kicks in so we can do more of what makes us feel good.

Too many goals

I have seen people with long lists of goals (sometimes more than 20) declaring they are going to have the most successful year ever. Invariably, they never achieve any of them. They become overwhelmed and unable to focus their efforts on any one thing because they are trying to achieve everything.

This goes against the very nature of setting a goal which implies that this is important and I want to give priority to it over other areas of my life. We cannot give priority to everything.

So what is the right number of goals? How many is too many?

There is no right answer to these questions. Everyone's capabilities are different. I suggest to my clients to take the lead from our brains.

Research shows that our brains are only capable of being aware of seven plus or minus two pieces of information at any one time.[10] In other words, short-term memory can only store between five and nine pieces of information that it has only been exposed to briefly. This is a good guide to use for goal setting. Focus on around five to seven goals at a time. More than seven runs the risk of being too many.

Remember, however, that the less goals we have, the more focused we can be in the allocation and investment of resources towards achieving that goal. Some may think that having only one goal and pouring all your resources into it is the best approach. I don't believe this to be the case for two reasons.

First, it limits our growth and potential. If you are passionate about developing your personal capacity and fulfilling your potential, then you should be growing and achieving in as many areas as you can without impeding on your performance.

Second, only having one goal has the potential to unbalance your work and life. This is the same result as only developing in one area of life (i.e. work) while neglecting others that are important (i.e. family and friends).

For those just starting out on this journey, I recommend starting with three goals in three different areas of life. Once you become effective in your goal setting and achievement, try increasing the number and see what works for you.

Reflection Time

1. Select a goal or aspiration you currently have and see if you can bring greater clarity to it by applying the SMARTPP formula.

2. What action could you take to increase the likelihood of achieving your goals?

CHAPTER EIGHT

The GROW Model

'You need to be a catalyst to push individuals to stretch and grow, and then provide safe opportunities for them to refine their skills'.
– Patrick McKenna and David Maister.

Up until now, we've been exploring the skill set of a coaching leader. We've looked at listening as laying the foundation for the relationship. We've looked at questions as the mechanics of coaching. We've looked at reframing and how we can ask specific types of questions in order to shift mindsets and make people more solution-focused and goal-oriented. We've looked at goal setting and getting super clear on what we want to achieve and the power of that clarity.

But how do we actually apply these skills and move through them in an effective order? The answer is the GROW Model.

The GROW Model was first published by Sir John Whitmore in his book *Coaching for Performance*,[1] when coaching made its debut in the corporate world. While there are many other models that are more modern and more comprehensive (and even arguably better), my aim here is not to produce high-quality executive coaches. My aim is to equip leaders to use coaching skills. So to keep it simple and effective, the GROW Model is an excellent choice.

The reality is that I still use the GROW Model more than any other when it comes to coaching conversations. It's the simplest model out there, and therefore the best when it comes to equipping leaders with coaching skills.

Understanding the GROW Model

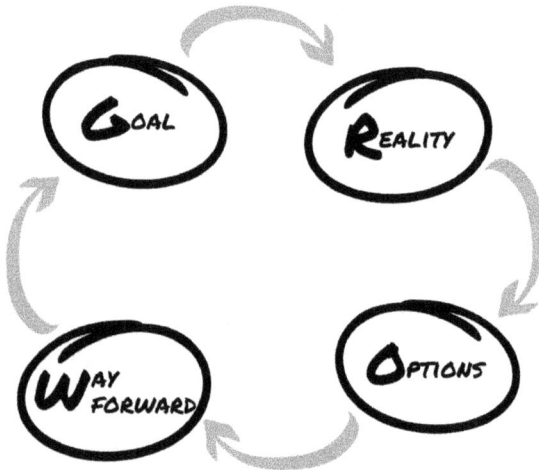

G is for 'goal'

Step one is to ask, what is your coachee's goal? Ask them – what are you trying to achieve? What outcome do you want? These are simple questions to ask, but often they're the hardest to answer.

I've lost count of the number of times I've asked a CEO, 'What is it you actually want?' and the answer is a blank stare. They've been so focused on the problem that they haven't actually thought about what they want out of the situation. So step one is to help them get really clear on what the situation is, and what they want to achieve.

This is again the principle of slowing it down at the front end, in order to speed it up at the back end. Slowing the coaching conversation down and taking your time to get crystal clear about what the goal is will speed up the back end of strategising the solution. It can be really hard to develop strategies and plan for a vague goal if you're not clear about what you want to achieve. Ask plenty of questions to try and achieve that clarity.

But it's more than just the result

Knowing the desired result is vital, but there are two other things that your coachee must get really clear on and that's the impact on people and impact on themselves.

1. **Impact on people**

   How do they want their people to feel when the result is achieved? There's no point setting high quarterly targets, then driving your team hard to meet them, if you then have broken and burnt-out people, or team members who no longer trust the leadership of the organisation.

   Too often we focus on the result and not on how we want people to feel at the end of the journey. And once we say, 'Hey, we want to get to this result, but we want people to feel satisfied, fulfilled, inspired at the end of it,' then we're going to go about it in a very different way.

2. **Impact on themselves**

   The other thing to explore here is how achieving their goal will actually make your coachee feel. What will it do for them? Is it going to make them feel inspired? Is it going to make them feel satisfied? Is it going to relieve a whole lot of negative emotion, stress, frustration, and anger that they're currently experiencing?

The value of exploring the emotional experience that's attached to a goal is that, in itself, it can be a really motivating factor. So when things get hard, they'll think, 'Remember, it's going to relieve this negative emotion, it's going to provide all this positive emotion.' We're attaching an emotional hook to the goal, which can be incredibly motivating.

R is for 'reality'

The second step of the GROW Model is to consider the reality your coachee is working in. What's the environment like? What's going on? What are all the factors contributing to the current situation? What are all the constraints within which they have to operate? What are the considerations they have to take into account as they formulate their plan?

The goal is where they want to go, while the reality is where they currently are. Until they understand where they *are* they won't be able to formulate a plan to move on. Once they do, then they can look at where they want to go and how to get there. That's the next stage of the conversation.

O is for 'options'

The third step is where we brainstorm and generate options to help the coachee get from where they are currently to where they want to be so they can actually achieve their goal.

Generally, when we ask people, 'What are the options that you've got to achieve your goal?', they can come up with three relatively easily. That's their 'easy thinking'. But the role of a coach and a coaching leader is to push people and encourage them to do the hard or critical thinking.

Research shows that critical thinking is an active process that uses subtle 'perception, analysis, synthesis and evaluation of information collected or derived from observation, experience, reflection, reasoning or communication'.[2] But most importantly, it's thinking that leads to action.[3] So critical thinking is not just thinking more deeply about a subject (or possible options), it's also about feeling committed to taking those thoughts and turning them into active steps.

In order to bring about this critical thinking when I'm coaching someone, I push them to move past the 'easy' three solutions and get at least seven ideas down. These are seven different options that they could take. And so often it's the sixth or the seventh idea that they come up with that is the best one. The reality is that the first idea they come up with is rarely their best. But it's never going to be their last, so pushing people to keep thinking is really important.

Of course, with this many ideas, don't expect every one of them to be great. At this stage I encourage people to put down any idea that comes to them – whether it's ridiculous or realistic, achievable or not. By putting it down, they're stimulating their creative juices.

Don't do the thinking for them

When I say it's stimulating their creative juices I do mean 'their'. Your role is to coach, not to come up with the ideas or to do their thinking for them.

As I've said before, part of coaching is to build up self-belief in people. If you're coaching one of your team, and you're the one coming up with the options, what's in it for them – even if your ideas succeed? On the other hand, if you coach leaders to come up with their own options, they'll be more motivated to implement them and, if their options ultimately succeed, they'll be the ones that get all the credit. And nothing builds self-belief like taking your own ideas to a successful, celebrated conclusion.

W is for 'way forward'

The final step is to develop the way forward – an action plan (and critical thinking will help to lead to this naturally). We evaluate different options, we see which one is the best. And then we come up with specific actions in order to implement those options.

Remember my mantra, 'The more specific you are, the more meaningful you become.' In this case, the more specific the action steps are, the more likely the leader is to go away and actually execute.

So, when I'm coaching a leader and I get to this stage of the conversation, I'll ask, 'OK, what are you going to do? Get really specific'. Once we have that nailed down I'll ask, 'So when are you going to take that action?' I'll get them to identify a specific date and time. The more specific I am with that, the more meaningful their commitment is and the more likely they are to go and actually implement and take action.

When they do, they get to tick that action item off the list, and they get a small dopamine hit. It's a win under the belt and it feels good. They want another one, so they think, 'What next?' Well, now they have at least three or four action items in their action plan, so they don't need to think about what the next item is – it's already written down.

They have a specific action item, ready and waiting with a specific date and time. So they pick one, implement it and they get to tick it off. Another small success, another dopamine hit, more good feelings. They want it again, so they repeat the process. And all of a sudden, they've built momentum. And momentum is a powerful thing.

Applying the GROW Model

Even though it's slightly simplistic, the GROW Model is powerful. It's a great way to coach your people.

As you saw in the GROW Model image that it is depicted in a circle. That's because, while the four stages of the model do follow on from each other, it's rarely a strictly linear process. You will jump between different stages of the model at different times of the coaching process.

You and your coachee may spend time clarifying what the goal is, and then come down and start talking about the reality but realise, as you talk, that what they saw as the core problem is not really the main issue. So you'll circle back to change the goal itself. This time, however, you no longer need to discuss the reality, because you've already done that. So you jump down to the option generation phase of the conversation.

Or you may be working on options and realise that there are, in fact, no options available. Your coachee just can't do anything to solve it. Everything is outside their control. So you may need to figure out whether or not this is the goal they should be working on, or whether there is something else within their control that they can focus on trying to achieve.

The GROW Model is also incredibly useful because of its flexibility. There are so many different ways it can be used. To this point, I've spoken about it in the context of a formal one-on-one coaching scenario, where you as a leader are speaking with one of your team, but it can be used in so many other ways.

GROW for collective problem solving

For example, the GROW Model is great as a collective problem solving tool. You can get together with your team, tackle a problem and go through each of the stages, just as you would in a one-on-one scenario. But you're doing it as a team, putting your combined brain power together to collaborate and come up with a workable action plan to solve the problem.

GROW for project planning

I know teams that use the GROW Model during the planning phase of different projects. Teams will ask themselves, 'What is the goal? What is the mission that we've got to achieve? What are the constraints in the environment that we're operating in, and what are the options that we've got to achieve that mission? What are we actually going to do?' It's a really effective planning tool for a project.

GROW for debriefing

Other teams use it as a tool for debriefing or reflection. At No.2 Flight Training School at RAAF Base Pearce, where all the Air Force pilots go as part of their training, they use the GROW Model to debrief after mission sorties.

They sit the pilots down and ask, 'What was the mission? OK, what actually happened? What options do we have for doing things differently? What could we have done differently this time, and what will we do differently next time? What's the lesson that we're going to take and apply in future?'

GROW for effective meetings

Others use the GROW Model to help run their meetings. I've worked with a number of teams who were finding their meetings a waste of time, walking out frustrated that nothing was achieved, despite people talking the entire time.

The GROW Model can bring a great structure to your meetings. 'The goal of this meeting is to come up with decisions A, B and C. So, what's the reality around decision A? What's the current environment, the context, the constraints, the considerations? All right, what options do we have, and what's the best option? What are we going to do to implement it? Now that we have the process, who's doing what? OK, let's repeat the process for decision B and C.' It's incredibly useful.

Conclusion

So, the GROW Model is a great model for coaching conversations. It works really well as a framework when we're helping individuals, but it's also applicable in so many situations outside of individual coaching.

Reflection time:

1. In what situations could you see yourself using the GROW model?

2. How confident do you feel about using the model in each of these situations?

3. What is one thing you could do to increase your level of confidence?

CHAPTER NINE

Practice

'*It is not the critic who counts; not the man who points out how the strong man stumbles, or where the doer of deeds could have done them better. The credit belongs to the man who is actually in the arena, whose face is marred by dust and sweat and blood; who strives valiantly; who errs, who comes short again and again, because there is no effort without error and shortcoming; but who does actually strive to do the deeds; who knows great enthusiasms, the great devotions; who spends himself in a worthy cause; who at the best knows in the end the triumph of high achievement, and who at the worst, if he fails, at least fails while daring greatly, so that his place shall never be with those cold and timid souls who neither know victory nor defeat.*'
– Theodore Roosevelt

I want to invite you to think about your leadership as a *practice*. The word practice can be either a verb or a noun. And both are applicable to leadership.

'Practise' as a verb

Let's start with practise as a verb – an action. It applies to leadership because leadership is a set of skills that can be learned. Historical research tells us that approximately 70% of leadership is developmental.[1] While this 70/20/10 model has been widely debunked – it's only the percentage that is up for debate – there is no dispute via researchers that learning occurs in leaders.[2]

Of course, there are also some characteristics such as personality and genetics that make people naturally charismatic – but this is only a portion (regardless of the percentage) of what makes up a leader's ability to influence others. The rest is made up of skills and behaviours that can be learned. And when something is *learned*, it must be practised.

As General Dwight D. Eisenhower famously said, 'The one quality that can be developed by studious reflection and practice is the leadership of men.'

'Practice' as a noun

A practice is also a professional pursuit. Doctors, lawyers and psychologists all operate a practice rather than a business. What is the difference? Well these are what we call 'professional industries'. And as professionals, these individuals are applying their expertise for the benefit of others. So, if a doctor or a lawyer were to move and begin working on the other side of the country, they take their 'practice' with them.

In the same way, as leaders we have a level of expertise and experience that we apply for the benefit of those we lead. And leaders also take their leadership expertise and experience with them when they change roles or organisations.

In the field of psychology, individuals are trained using what is known as the scientist-practitioner model. This involves training as both scientists who can use the scientific methods to conduct research, and as practitioners who can practise the application of science in the real world. While there are some who spend their career straddling both research and practice, most specialise, becoming either a researcher and academic or a practitioner.

I am a practitioner of psychology. I don't just think about it, study it and write about it. I practise it. And I embrace leadership in the same way. I'm a practitioner of leadership and I practise it every day.

3 elements of a leadership practice

To operate a leadership practice, there are three things you need to do.

1. Take action
2. Pursue mastery
3. Join the profession

1. Take action

When you Google the word practice, the following definitions appear:

1. The actual application or use of an idea, belief, or method, as opposed to theories relating to it.
2. The customary, habitual, or expected procedure or way of doing something.
3. Repeated exercise in or performance of an activity or skill so as to acquire or maintain proficiency in it.

I also love how the Cambridge Dictionary defines 'practice' simply as, 'action, rather than thought or ideas.'

You can see the theme that emerges from these definitions. It is one of action and application. Leadership is not about theorising how to influence people and achieve goals. While theorising, reflecting and conceptualising what effective leadership looks like is an important part of the learning process, real leadership is about actually taking action and achieving results.

I love Peter Drucker's (one of the most widely-known and influential thinkers on management) perspective on this when he says, 'Effective leadership is not about making speeches or being liked; leadership is defined by results, not by attributes.'

'Leadership is practised not so much in words as in attitudes and actions.'
– Harold S. Green

2. Pursue mastery

The next step in leadership practice is to pursue mastery. A practitioner is someone who always seeks to develop – or even master – their practice. To do this, they are continually learning, honing their skills and seeking to enhance their abilities. They are intentional about their practice, monitoring and reflecting on their performance, learning from mistakes, identifying improvements and seeking to apply these insights at the next opportunity.

Max De Pree – who as CEO of Herman Miller, Inc. took the small family run business to one of the most profitable Fortune 500 companies in the world – famously described leadership as an art.[3] When combined with our earlier definition that leadership is about influencing people, you might say that leadership is the art of influencing people.

Mastery of the art of leadership is not only the development and use of leadership skills – it's also knowing which skills to use when and being able to tailor their application to the context in which you are leading in. Just as a master painter would choose different brushes, paints and colour combinations to achieve the desired effect in a painting, a great leader will choose to demonstrate different behaviours, communicate in different ways and adopt different approaches according to the individual or teams they wish to influence.

3. Join the profession

This third element is all about shifting your mindset and bringing a level of professionalism to your leadership. According to the Professional Standards Council, 'a profession positions itself as possessing special knowledge and skills... [and] is prepared to apply this knowledge and exercise these skills in the interest of others'.[4]

A 'profession' is also made up of professionals. A professional is someone paid for their skills and expertise in a particular area. If you are reading this and you have supervisory, managerial or leadership responsibilities as part of your employment, you meet this definition. You are being paid to lead. You are a professional leader. The question is, are you being professional about your leadership?

Most people adopt a professional identity that is industry-centric. They consider themselves a nurse, an accountant, an engineer or an IT professional first, who has leadership responsibilities second. But the world needs more professional leaders (who see themselves as leaders first) who then operate in their chosen industries.

While you may not belong to a formal professional group such as the Institute of Managers and Leaders or the National Society of Leadership and Success (yes there is such a thing!), thinking of yourself as part of the broader leadership profession will help bring a level of professionalism to your leadership practice and set you apart from others in your industry. And if you are not yet paid for your leadership contribution, adopting the mindset and practice of a professional is more important. Embodying the qualities and practice of a professional will eventually result in someone providing you with the opportunity to generate an income as a leader.

The coaching leader is a practitioner of leadership first and foremost – even before their industry profession. At the same time, they are practitioners of coaching as well. Their leadership practice is built around coaching those they lead. They seek to practise the use of coaching skills, developing a level of expertise (without trying to become an expert executive coach) in their application as they lead and develop their people. In doing so they truly become professional leaders and developers of individual and organisational capability.

There may be (and should be) times when you formally coach your staff one-on-one. However, if this is the only scenario where you are seeking to apply coaching skills, you are limiting yourself and your effectiveness.

As you go about the day-to-day practise of leadership, you will, if you are looking for them, identify plenty of opportunities to apply coaching skills. As a coaching leader, you should be using your coaching skills in many of your daily interactions with your team. In fact, there are very few leadership activities that can't be enhanced using coaching skills. Whether that is self-coaching in preparation for the task or by using coaching skills to develop and engage with people.

However, it is always helpful to understand the key opportunities where you may apply coaching to your leadership. And while the below is not an exhaustive list, these are the opportunities that I have found while working with leaders that have provided some of the greatest benefits from coaching.

🔍 Reflection time

1. Do you consider yourself to be a professional leader?

2. If you began to consider yourself a professional leader, what would change for you?

Key coaching opportunities

There are many different opportunities for a leader to coach their people. Listed here are a number of key examples of where a leader might employ coaching skills with their people.

Formal coaching

Where possible it's good practise for leaders and managers to be meeting one-on-one regularly with their direct reports. While different workplaces and working arrangements will determine the nature and frequency of these meetings, it should be no less than monthly. And ideally more frequently.

These one-on-ones are great opportunities for formal coaching to occur. You can address challenges of specific projects, brainstorm how an individual might shift their performance from good to great or even help staff achieve further career aspirations. Whatever the subject matter, these are prime opportunities to formally coach for personal and professional development.

While formal coaching can be incorporated into the regular battle rhythm of your team, there are also times when it can be used to great effect to deal with short-term issues as they arrive. Over the years in various leadership roles, I've held coaching and mentoring sessions with members of my teams to deal with seasonal workload and stress, conflict with colleagues, challenges relating to current projects and many other specific issues. Usually only one to three sessions are needed on top of business as usual to support team members.

I've also conducted (and received coaching in) longer-term coaching arrangements. This could be a bi-monthly or quarterly arrangement to aid with personal growth and progression towards long-term ambitions. In such arrangements, often it can be beneficial for individuals to gain an external perspective. This could mean receiving coaching from a competent leader from another team/department within your organisation (e.g., Level 4 or 5 coaching leader) or with an external professional.

Informal coaching

The more intentional you are about coaching your people, the more you will find a coaching approach begins to creep into your day-to-day interactions with your staff. I remember a conversation in a carpark one afternoon. As I arrived, I passed a woman I knew as she was leaving. We said hello and I enquired about her day. She expressed some frustration about it not being as productive as she would have liked.

So I asked her what would have made it more productive for her. She stopped and thought about it for a moment before answering. As she did, I could see she had a light bulb go on inside – that look when the penny drops and insight is gained. I love that look. So I followed up by asking her what she thought she could do the next day. She rattled off a couple of things, we said goodbye and went our separate ways.

The whole conversation took less than five minutes. But she walked away with a new approach to her day. And I walked away smiling knowing I had just coached her and she didn't even know it. Whether making a cup of coffee, over lunch or returning to your desk from a meeting, you will find plenty of opportunities to informally coach people – if you are looking for them.

Meetings

Meetings are another opportunity for leaders to regularly coach and use coaching skills. Whether it's a planning meeting, a project meeting or a regular team meeting, there are plenty of opportunities within any meeting for a leader to use coaching skills to enhance the outcomes of the meeting. And because the entire team benefits, coaching during meetings also provides great ROI.

So how does coaching look in the meeting environment? First, coaching in a meeting begins with having clearly defined outcomes. This is then followed by good strategic questions which help facilitate collaborative conversation and collective insight to achieve those outcomes.

In a meeting a coaching leader will also need to be intentional about coaching for learning. One of the key characteristics of high-performing teams is that they are teams that learn. A good leader will make a habit of facilitating reflection and review of the team's performance to identify the lessons from activities or time periods so they can be articulated and implemented in the future.

Coaching leaders aren't only intentional about doing this themselves, they are also intentional about teaching and coaching team members how to both run meetings and facilitate team learning. In this way they are coaching others to coach in a meeting setting and being intentional about developing this capability across the team.

Decision making

One thing leaders need to do regularly is make decisions. But many leaders erroneously think the decision-making process is up to them and them alone. This not only places a whole lot of pressure on the leader to come up with the best decision, it also limits the amount of input they can put into the decision. Additionally, leaders who lock themselves in their office and make decisions by themselves fail to develop people and capability within the organisation.

A coaching leader is likely to take a different approach. They understand that the decision-making process can be enhanced by coaching and that having coaching skills and the ability to self-coach is a vital part of making better decisions. So, when faced with a decision that needs to be made or a plan that needs to be developed, their default position leads them to invite one or two of their people into their office and include them in the process. After explaining the scenario and the decision that needs to be made, they might then ask, 'What would you do?'

The team member then begins to outline the approach they would take. This then becomes an opportunity to coach them through the decision-making process. They might ask questions like:

- What is the end outcome we really want to achieve?

- What are the key considerations at play?

- What are the different options available?

- Which one do you think is the best option?

- What are the implications for the team?

- What are the implications for the broader organisation?

- What would your decision be?

At the end of the conversation the leader thanks their team member and once they leave, sits down to finalise their decision.

Let's consider the benefits to this approach.

- **It helps inform the leader's decision-making process.** The leader is now getting another person's input and perspective into the situation. They are using two brains, rather than just their own. Often this will bring additional information or highlight alternate perspectives not initially considered by the leader.

- **It clarifies the leader's thinking.** Coaching leaders understand that clarity around an issue comes not only from being coached, but also by coaching others on that same issue. By helping others articulate their thoughts in order to find clarity, the leaders own thoughts and thought processes are clarified.

- **It builds trust and respect.** Including people in, and allowing them to contribute to, decision-making - something traditionally seen as the responsibility of leaders – makes people feel special. To be trusted enough to contribute to a leader's decisions, inspires reciprocal trust in return. Including people in a decision-making process is not something insecure leaders would do. Doing so demonstrates a level of security in the leader's identity and role, which will generate respect.

- **It provides insight into operating at the next level.** When individuals are included in the decision-making and planning conducted by their leaders, they gain a greater appreciation of what is required to operate at the next level. This provides them with an insight into the way their leader thinks, what considerations they need to take into account and a greater understanding of the leader's priorities. This insight itself has a number of benefits:

  ° It helps develop the team member's strategic thinking and decision-making capability.

  ° It helps the individual involved accept, support and explain the leader's decision with other team members because they have insight into the decision-making journey.

  ° It helps team members understand how they can support their leader and understand some of the complexity and pressure their leader faces.

  ° It helps individuals be more motivated and intentional about how they can develop their own capability to be able to operate at the next level and progress in their career.

  ° It helps the leader get to know their people further. It helps them understand how they think, what their decision-making processes are and what level of leadership capability they have. This also allows the leader to identify development needs for their people.

One-up training

The inclusion of people in the decision-making process by leaders is a form of one-up training. One-up training is the practice of being trained and gaining experience by operating in a role that is one up from your current position. This is a common practice within military organisations where there is a requirement for individuals to be able to step up and lead under pressure at a moment's notice should a leader be lost on the battlefield.

However there doesn't need to be the threat of leaders being killed suddenly to adopt this approach. Regardless of the industry or organisation you find yourself in, this approach is an informal but excellent method of talent management and succession planning.

Should a leader be promoted, take leave or move on, this practice ensures there are team members ready to fill the role providing a level of consistency for the organisation, reducing recruiting and on-boarding costs and decreasing lost opportunity costs associated with new leaders getting up to speed.

Coaching enhances feedback effectiveness

One of the great ways that leaders use coaching skills to enhance the way they lead is to apply these skills when they deliver feedback to their staff. There are three main benefits from doing so. The first is that you engage them in the process. The second is that you increase your empathy. The third is that you increase their ownership.

A 4-step formula for delivering feedback

Before we jump into the benefits of using coaching skills to deliver feedback, a couple of notes on delivering effective feedback in general. When most leaders deliver feedback it goes something like this: 'This is what you did wrong and this is what you need to do to improve in the future.'

When I teach leaders to deliver effective feedback, I offer them a four-step formula.

Step 1. Ask

This is where we ask for permission to deliver the feedback. It's simply a statement such as, 'Hey can I give you a piece of feedback?' But it's an important initial step because it communicates respect, which can diffuse defences, laying an important foundation for delivering feedback.

If people are not in the right mindset or mental space to receive feedback, trying to push forward and deliver it at that time is more likely to do more damage than good. Your feedback simply won't achieve the intent of developing the individual. So asking in order to communicate respect and make sure they're ready for the feedback is the first step.

Step 2. Observation

Provide an observation. This must be very concise, objectively stating what was observed without emotion or judgement. For an example you might say, 'John, I've noticed over the past three weeks you've been consistently late to the management meeting.'

Step 3. Impact

The third step is discussing the impact of the behaviour, situation or whatever the subject of the feedback is. This is the part of the feedback process that is most often skipped by leaders but it's actually the most important part. And that's because this is where we discuss the *why* behind the change that's needed. When people understand the why behind the change, they're much more likely to be proactive in engaging with and making the change.

Step 4. Solution

The final step then is to conceptualise solutions. Here we are asking what is the solution or change that can remedy the specific scenario that we're addressing.

Now let's explore what happens when we use coaching questions when delivering feedback.

Benefits of using coaching questions when delivering feedback

Engaging them in the process

When you fail to engage your team in the coaching process, then you are simply 'doing *to* versus doing *with*'. This is the sibling of telling versus asking. Unfortunately this approach occurs all too often with leaders delivering feedback by pointing out to people, 'This is what you've done wrong and this is what you need to do.' However, when we deliver feedback in a directive or telling manner, our staff are passive. They're simply sitting there listening to what is being said and having feedback delivered to them.

On the other hand, by asking strategic questions and applying coaching skills throughout the feedback process, we can actually get our staff to engage their brains and take action. They become collaborators and co-creators in the feedback process. Our coaching questions encourage them to participate and actively think about and engage with the content of the feedback in the moment.

This makes the process so much more effective and increases the likelihood of our staff getting valuable insights and connecting with lessons that they can apply in the future.

Increasing empathy

The second benefit of using coaching skills when delivering feedback is its ability to increase empathy. Empathy is essentially the ability to put yourself in somebody else's shoes – to imagine and identify with the experience of others. When we ask questions at each stage of the feedback process it helps us to develop empathy.

During the observation stage we might ask, 'What do you think I observed?' Or, 'What do you think others saw during those circumstances?' In asking these questions we're encouraging people to reflect from the perspective of others.

In the impact stage of feedback, we might ask questions like, 'What do you think the impact for that particular person was?', 'How do you think that behaviour made that person feel?' or, 'What do you think the thought process of the individual involved might have been?'

These kinds of questions encourage our people to adopt or to actively think about the experience of others in response to their own behaviour. In doing so they are developing the empathy muscle.

Increasing ownership

The final benefit of using coaching skills and strategic questions when delivering feedback is that it increases ownership over the individual's behaviour, the outcomes from that behaviour and also the future solutions and changes that need to be made. When we are exploring what changes might be made or solutions implemented and we coach people to identify those solutions rather than tell them what needs to be done, this is far more likely to increase ownership. And that has the additional result of increasing their implementation of any action plans developed.

A number of years ago I was leading a team where there was some conflict between two of my team members. I distinctly remember having a conversation with one of them where I was providing feedback about their contribution to the conflict.

During that conversation I asked her a series of questions to first get her to consider things from the other party's perspective, taking into account the level of experience (or in this case lack thereof) of the other person involved. I followed these questions up with asking about the impacts of her behaviour, and how her behaviour might be perceived by the other person. I asked how she thought they might feel and whether or not that was conducive to an effective working relationship.

I remember seeing the look on her face as she had that lightbulb moment and gained the insight I was hoping she would find. As a result of that conversation, she was able to identify what she needed to do in order to repair the relationship and facilitate effective collaboration moving forward.

Coaching skills increase effectiveness

Using coaching skills when delivering feedback powerfully increases the effectiveness of leaders across a variety of industries. One 2019 study showed coaching by supervisors before delivery of performance feedback not only boosted work engagement among staff but also decreased turnover.[5]

These findings were supported by another study in the manufacturing industry where 20 managers took part in a 360-degree feedback process.[6] Those that received coaching with their feedback were shown to have a decrease in rating discrepancy between their self-assessment and the assessments of others.[7]

The analysis of this study was able to show the decrease in rating discrepancy was due to an increase of the performance ratings of others and not a decrease in their own self-ratings due to an increase in self-awareness.[8] In other words, others viewed the manager in a better light. The associated benefits in this study demonstrated an increase in staff satisfaction, increased organisational commitment amongst team members and again a decrease in turnover intention.[9]

The results of both studies show how important coaching skills are when delivering performance feedback. They increase the effectiveness of that feedback, and they also identify and articulate how the use of coaching skills by leaders addresses the very real problem they face with the war for talent and keeping and retaining the people that will make their teams and companies successful in today's world.

Small corrections

When it comes to feedback, we need to be giving it constantly. A small change early is often easy to make. But the longer a behaviour or habit is allowed to continue, the more entrenched it becomes and the harder it is to change. And this can then lead to 'normalised deviation'.

The normalisation of deviance was first introduced by sociologist Diane Vaughan in response to the US Challenger disaster.[10] In reviewing that event, Vaughan found that the root cause of the disaster was due to the fact that NASA officials continued to fly the space shuttle despite a design flaw with the O-rings. Because they made that repeated choice, it became 'normal' – the team simply undertook the deviant practice as an acceptable choice.

The longer deviant behaviours are left unaddressed in any team, the further the deviation from what is expected and the more normalised it becomes. Once this happens, it requires significantly more time, energy and effort to change. In the workplace, this sucks a significant amount of attention away from core performance activities – both on the part of the individual who must make the change, but also the leader who has to keep the individual.

In many ways it's like the skilful driving of a car. When you first learn to drive, you learn to continually make small adjustments to the steering wheel and avoid big jerks and turns to get you where you want to go. In the same way, if we are having small feedback conversations all the time with our people, then we'll be consistently making small corrections to stay aligned with our expectations.

And just like in a car, the faster you go, the more important continual smaller corrections become. A small deviation at 50km/hr may take 15 to '20 seconds before the car leaves the road. The same deviation at 100km/hr may result in a crash in only three seconds. In the fast paced world we live in, the requirement for regular feedback has never been greater.

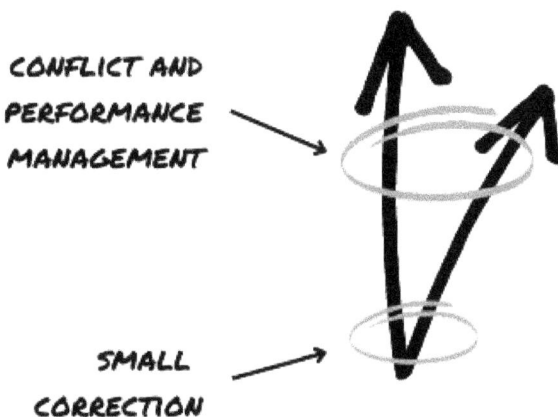

CONFLICT AND
PERFORMANCE
MANAGEMENT

SMALL
CORRECTION

A series of small changes are not only easier for our staff to make, they are also easier for leaders to instigate. It's much easier to have a two-minute feedback conversation than to have a lengthy discussion about significant changes that are required. The longer we wait to provide feedback, the harder it becomes.

When issues are left unaddressed and significant behavioural deviations uncorrected, eventually the impacts begin to substantially affect the performance of the individual and team. At this point leaders are forced to intervene resulting in difficult conversations and sometimes formal performance management is required.

Small corrections prevent large deviations that result in conflict and difficult conversations.

Performance management

In the vast majority of cases performance management can be avoided by early and regular feedback. However the reality is that at some stage every leader is going to be required to performance manage their staff. When we do, coaching skills can once again enhance the process.

Start with the purpose

As with any process, it's always important to start with the purpose in order to figure out the best way to conduct it. The purpose of performance management is to provide underperforming staff with the opportunity to lift their game and meet the minimum standards required in the workplace.

The optimal outcome for any performance management conversation is that the individual team member involved walks away with absolute clarity. Clarity about the standards they are required to meet, the behaviours they are required to display and what they need to do to improve their performance. They should also leave the conversation with clarity about the consequences of not performing. Ideally, they would walk away with a sense of ownership of their plan and responsibility for their performance.

An opportunity not a punishment

As a coaching leader we're looking to develop our people in everything they do. Because of that, we cannot approach these scenarios from a punitive perspective. We cannot use the process to threaten our staff into performing. Instead we have to view performance management as another opportunity to develop an underperforming staff member, albeit in a more formal and serious manner.

Preparation

One of the keys to successful performance management is preparation. As James Baker, former Secretary of State said, 'Proper preparation prevents poor performance'. The preparation for performance management conversations is an opportunity for leaders to self-coach.

A great place to start would be to consider what questions you would ask a leader in your team if you were going to coach them through performance managing one of their own team members. Write those down and answer those yourself. Having coached many leaders through this process, I recommend considering the following questions:

- What do I want the outcome of this conversation to be?

- What do I want them to understand?

- What do I want them to do at the end of the conversation?

- How do I want them to feel at the end of the conversation?

- How do I have the conversation in a way that ensures they understand what they need to?

Understanding the outcome you want

Understanding the outcome you want is an important part of determining how to conduct the rest of the conversation.

In the case where the underperforming individual is a good person and has plenty of potential, the desired outcome is that they respond positively, improve their performance and continue being a valuable team member. In that case you want them to walk away with a clear action plan, feeling valued, supported and motivated to improve. Identifying this up front allows you to plan how you will frame the conversation and decide what language you will use to achieve this outcome.

To think this is the case every time however, is naïve and unrealistic. There are times when you will find yourself leading people who are not conducive to building high-performing teams and good cultures. These people may be lazy, they may be unethical or they may be good people who simply do not have what it takes to perform in their current role. In some rare cases they may be truly malevolent individuals.

Whatever the reason, keeping underperforming individuals in the workplace will not only hamper team performance, it will destroy the motivation of others and erode trust in your leadership. Research also shows that it impacts on your other employees' stress levels and creates more turnover.[11] As Perry Belcher writes, 'Nothing will kill a great employee faster than watching you tolerate a bad one.'

A good leader – whether they coach or not – will always seek to manage those individuals not conducive to high performance and healthy cultures out of the organisation. Coaching leaders are not afraid of doing so. They are just likely to use questioning as part of the process of doing so.

Having the conversation

The best way for leaders to have performance management conversations is highly dependent on the context. This includes the organisational requirements, the individuals involved and the issues at hand. If, as a leader, you're looking for advice regarding how to best conduct these conversations, I recommend seeking guidance from your leadership, your HR function or a mentor familiar with your context.

However you seek to approach it, coaching skills can help. Remember that coaching is fundamentally about inspiring change and the purpose of performance management is to provide the opportunity for an individual to lift their performance. At the end of the conversation, you want them to walk away and change their approach to work.

So as you have the conversation, consider what the individual needs to become aware of to change their behaviour and performance. How can you use coaching skills to raise the individual's awareness?

Do they need to become aware of the impact of their lack of performance on others, the team and the company? Do they need to become aware of the perception others have of them? Or do they need to become aware of the consequences of not changing?

Additionally, consider what needs to happen to raise the level of responsibility in the individual? Does the individual need to take responsibility for aspects of their role previously unattended to? How do you have the conversation to increase the chance that they'll take responsibility for the action plan that will result from the conversation?

While considering these questions may form part of your preparation, asking strategic questions to help raise awareness and responsibility throughout the conversation will help enhance the engagement throughout.

Another coaching technique that is often useful in these scenarios is having the individual repeat back key insights and the action plan as the conversation draws to a close. This is something that many coaches do in coaching sessions to summarise the session and ensure that both the coach and coachee are on the same page regarding what will happen moving forward. For the same reason, it's a good practice to help wrap up performance management conversations.

The follow up

Performance management is never just a single conversation. It is a process that requires multiple touch points, discussions and performance reviews. Using coaching skills to help facilitate reflection by the individual in question on their own performance helps keep them engaged in the process and helps model the process they should ideally be conducting themselves on a regular basis.

Having them identify where they are and how they can improve further, as well as asking them to develop their own action plans to meet and exceed the required performance standards will increase the likelihood they will feel empowered during the process. Even better, it will motivate them to own the outcome of the process.

Remember that the key outcome for a successful performance management conversation is the individual walking away with absolute clarity regarding what is required from them to meet the required standards. Leaders need to be mindful not to sacrifice this outcome for the sake of coaching. If you are still learning how to coach or are inexperienced having these conversations, relying on telling rather than asking may help you achieve the clarity required.

If this is the case, that's OK. At the same time, by inserting strategic questions throughout your performance management conversations, you have the ability to get the outcome you want in a way that develops awareness, responsibility and self-belief. This increases the likelihood that the individual will make positive changes which will support the development of future capability and performance.

When not to coach

After reading everything in this book so far, you might be thinking that I see coaching as the be all and end all. You might think that I believe leaders should be coaching in every circumstance. That is definitely not the case. There are times when coaching is simply not appropriate.

Here are four situations where coaching is not the most effective approach.

Situation 1: Where there is low knowledge, skills and experience

For coaching to be successful it requires a baseline level of skills, knowledge and experience. Coaching leverages the knowledge and skills an individual already has in order to grow their capabilities further. Without baseline knowledge or skills there is nothing to leverage.

As a weapons instructor, if I was working with a new recruit who was handling a weapon for the very first time and who had no knowledge of how to handle a weapon in a safe manner, trying to coach them would not only be ineffective, it would also be dangerous.

Situation 2: When there is imminent danger

When I was learning to drive as a teenager I took lessons with a driving instructor whose vehicle had dual controls. While there was still only one steering wheel located in the driver's seat, the passenger seat of this vehicle had a clutch and brake and accelerator pedals. This allowed the instructor to demonstrate effective pedal operation and also take control of the vehicle in an emergency.

During my first lesson, the car in front of us slammed on its brakes suddenly. I responded more slowly than I should have, resulting in the instructor slamming on the brakes and stopping the car himself. If instead he had stopped to ask me if I was responding quickly enough or if I should be braking harder, we would have had an accident. Instead, he simply took control to ensure we were safe.

In situations where there is imminent danger, it can be irresponsible for leaders to try to coach. It is far more appropriate for them to take control and give direction.

Situation 3: When time is of the essence

The reality is that coaching does take time. There is an investment required to slow down, ask questions and draw the answers out of people. However, there are times when deadlines are looming and the consequences of not meeting those deadlines may be severe. In those situations the short-term consequences may outweigh the long-term benefits of making the time investment required for coaching.

In such scenarios reverting to directing may provide faster results and thereby greater benefit to the team. And while I readily acknowledge the existence of these scenarios, I would argue they are much rarer than leaders realise. Most leaders have much more time than they think.

Situation 4: When people aren't in the right headspace

The very nature of asking questions and trying to get people to think increases the cognitive load or the amount of mental work the people have to do. But individuals under high amounts of stress and pressure are already experiencing significant cognitive load. Under such levels of pressure, an individual's executive function in the brain is reduced and their ability to think clearly and to learn is diminished.

Coaching in these scenarios has the potential to cause greater levels of frustration and increased feelings of futility as people struggle to come up with sufficient answers to the questions that they're being asked. This reduces their level of self-belief and has the potential to increase their mental strain and create negative consequences for their wellbeing. It also has the potential of damaging the relationship with the leader, eroding trust rather than building it.

But... coaching reigns supreme

This being said, outside of these four scenarios a coaching approach is the best default approach for leaders to adopt. If the primary objectives of a leader are to achieve results from those they lead and also develop capability within those they lead, adopting an approach that achieves both objectives simultaneously is more effective and efficient than pursuing each in isolation.

Coaching is an approach that does this and delivers all those benefits. So, it stands to reason that this approach should be the leader's default and deviating from it should occur only by exception.

No time to coach

It's not uncommon for me to have leaders turn around and say, 'Cliff this sounds great and I want to be able to do this but I just don't have the time. If I take the time to coach my people, I won't get all my work done.'

It's true that leaders these days are under incredible pressure with higher workloads than ever before. However, trying to achieve as much as you can as fast as you can without trying to reduce the workload over time is a recipe for burnout and eventual failure. Leaders who take this approach end up trapped in the tyranny of the urgent, failing to focus on the important things that sustain success. They become so focused on solving the short-term problems in front of them they lose sight of the benefits of pursuing the long-term rewards of developing people and capability. This short-sighted view keeps them focused on removing their present pain but at the expense of pursuing future gain.

Author James Clear writes, '[I]n the long run, prioritisation beats efficiency'.[12] This is a lesson I learned in my early 20s when I sat down with a leader I was working under and asked him how he carried so much responsibility. Given the number of portfolios he oversaw, I was keen to learn how he did it all. He indicated that he sat down each week and asked himself the question, 'What can I do today that is going to give me more time in six weeks?'

Answering that question helped him to focus on what was most important in achieving long-term sustainable success rather than having a reactive approach where he was just tackling the latest email in his inbox. He was taking steps to reduce his future workload so he could pursue more important things.

This leader also told me that often the answer to that question was something inconvenient and required a sacrifice from him. So often this is the case. Taking the time to coach can be inconvenient and can slow things down. However, the rewards over time speed things up and provide us with more time in the future.

My first business coach, Wez Hone, taught me that when you slow it down at the front end, you speed it up at the back end. While he taught this principle primarily in the context of sales and customer experience, it's a principle that applies in leadership and developing people as well. When a leader takes the time to slow down and make the investment in coaching their people, the result is increased capability, initiative, motivation and autonomy that eventually speeds up their performance and gives their leader more time.

In the early days of my involvement with the Air Force Leadership Coaching Program, I was running a workshop training leaders in the use of coaching skills. That's when I met two sergeants who together managed a warehouse full of aircraft technicians.

As it happened this particular group of aircraft technicians were quite a junior workforce and the sergeants found themselves constantly being asked what to do and how to solve problems. The result was that they were spending the majority of their day responding to the queries of their staff rather than doing the specific management work that was required of them. They were often stuck working after hours or taking work home with them in order to get all their tasks completed. And this was leading them on the road to burn out.

After sitting in on the training I had run, they both decided to intentionally apply a coaching approach with their staff. Instead of just answering the questions of their junior technicians, they began coaching and responding with questions of their own. After a number of weeks the technicians began to wonder about the different approach. They asked, 'Serge, how come you never give us the answers anymore? All you do is ask us all these questions!'

The sergeants brought everybody together and explained what coaching was and what they were trying to achieve. Once the technicians understood the process, they willingly and intentionally engaged with it. Within six weeks the entire environment within the workshop had turned around. Morale was higher, maintenance turnaround times were faster and other performance metrics had increased. The greatest benefit for the sergeants, however, was that they now had time to complete their own work during their work day.

So when I encounter leaders who tell me they don't have time to coach, my response is always, 'How do you have time not to coach?!'

Planning your coaching practice

Hopefully this chapter has inspired you to consider how you might be able to use coaching to enhance your leadership practice. The key is being intentional about keeping the concept of coaching in front of mind especially as you get sucked into the vortex of your work.

If you are just starting out, consider planning out your week. Sit down at the start of the week and consider what opportunities you may have coming up in the week ahead where you could coach your people. Pick two or three and focus your efforts. Or you might want to pick one opportunity each day and make it a daily practice. The more you do it, the more you will naturally and instinctively begin to identify opportunities to coach in the moment.

If you are a seasoned leader who has been coaching for a while, I encourage you to take the time to consider the additional opportunities you might have to coach those you lead. That might involve teaching them a coaching skill or two and providing an opportunity to use it. Doing so will help you continue to progress to the next level on your journey as a coaching leader.

Reflection time

1. Which areas of your leadership will you begin to practice coaching skills?

2. When do you start?

CHAPTER TEN

The art of coaching up

'Coaching your boss, or other leaders beyond that, can be a tricky business...You cannot become a true change agent until you develop this capability.'
– Jamie Flinchbaugh

John Baldoni in his book, *Lead Your Boss*, writes, 'The boss needs someone who can think through what is happening and what is not happening. It's a mindset that leaders can learn to develop in themselves and in others. Taking time to think before acting prevents going down blind alleys'.[1]

A good leader loves to have the support of those who they lead. They recognise that they cannot do everything themselves. And if they had to, the result would never be as good as if they did it with the support of those they lead. Great leaders need to be surrounded by competent proactive individuals who think through situations, identify solutions and develop action plans independently; those who shoulder the burden of leadership and reduce the workload of their leader.

At the same time, leaders very rarely like to be told what to do by those they lead. They are often confident and competent in their own ability – which are the same traits that make them good leaders. But it's also these qualities that can result in negative reactions from the leader when they are challenged by their staff.

The coaching leader's practice is about the opportunities they have to apply coaching in their leadership. Coaching up is one of those opportunities.

What is coaching up?

'Coaching up' is using the learning and methods from coaching and communication skills to promote productive relationships with leaders who can influence our future success. And like the name indicates, it's the process of a team member using coaching skills with their leaders.

Coaching up can be a bit like an early warning detection system on a ship. When the system radar picks up danger ahead it doesn't automatically change the course of the ship. Instead it alerts the captain to the potential danger ahead, allowing the captain to change course.

In this scenario the captain maintains control of the ship, but the early warning system influences the course of the ship and gives input that informs the captain's decision. The end result is that the captain and the ship are able to avoid disaster.

The art of coaching up works in much the same way. It influences a leader's decision making while still allowing them to maintain control and authority. It's a guiding light rather than an overshadowing one, helping leaders to see the way to becoming more effective and better leaders overall.

Research shows that great leaders are the ones that incorporate diverse views while supporting skilful conversations and open dialogue with their teams and those they lead.[2] These great leaders are embracing the process of coaching up.

The effectiveness of coaching up

Coaching up can be a very effective process for both leaders and staff. A story I read in Success in LiveChat from leader and editor, Brendan Heffernan, demonstrates this very well:

My first, and probably biggest, mistake is that I assumed my leadership style worked for everyone on my team and that they would have to adjust to my style because I was in charge. This obviously couldn't have been further from the truth as I know now. We were organizing a jobs boot camp once with around ten job seekers and 20 potential employers where the goal was to coordinate a networking event to surround these recent college graduates with ideal companies to network with. While organizing this event, I had to manage my team through multiple stages of the process and realized quickly that everyone didn't flow the same.

My approach is very no-nonsense and, if I see someone joking around, I immediately think they aren't taking the task seriously. One person on the team is not that way and jokes a lot. So much so that I had to address her early in the project and was met with resistance. She didn't think the project had to be as serious as I was making it out to be, and eventually, I realized that she was right, and I was wrong.

She worked with our businesses through the process, and I realized that if she had her head down and acted as no-nonsense as me, she wouldn't have as good a relationship with her contacts, thus making it harder for us to find good companies to participate.[3]

While this began as a conflict situation, Brendan was able to take the team member's ideas and situation on board to make changes that ultimately benefited the entire company.

Of course, we don't want to start out our coaching up with a conflict if it can be helped. Choosing our moments and our scenarios for coaching up is an important part of the process because it allows you *and* your leader to be prepared for change.

There are two main scenarios where I find coaching up to be the most effective. The first is where a leader needs to gain clarity and alignment. The second is where a leader needs to change a problematic course of action.

Scenario 1: Gaining clarity and alignment

It's not uncommon for leaders to delegate tasks and initiatives believing that they've been super clear in their communication about what is needed and expected when in reality they've left those team members receiving the instruction confused or with questions. The use of coaching skills by the team member can be an effective way of gaining both clarity and alignment moving forward.

Just as coaching helps individuals to see themselves more clearly, coaching up helps leaders see themselves (and their leadership) more clearly. It provides a method for them to receive feedback that encourages reflection, learning and growth. It also helps them to see how and where they spend their time, and how this may (or may not) diverge from their values or goals for the team and organisation.

So, the process of coaching up can bring clarity to both the team member, who now understands their tasks or responsibilities better, and the leader, who now understands themselves and their leadership skills better.

Team members who find themselves in a situation of 'coaching up' to gain more clarity from their leader might consider the following four questions:

Style 1: Hey boss. Thanks for that. I just want to ask a couple of questions to ensure we're both on the same page moving forward. Based on what you just said the goal of this new initiative is...[insert goal]. Is that right?

Style 2: Given the current environment I would expect that major considerations when developing a plan would be... [insert considerations]. Are there any others that I've missed?

Style 3: I came up with a number of options that I thought were viable. The best ones were... [insert options]. Are there any others I haven't thought of?

Style 4: In my view the best option is... [insert option] and the first steps I would take to implement that course of action are... [insert action plan]. Are you happy with that plan?

At this stage you will likely recognise that these four questions are designed around the GROW model. In asking them you have clarified:

- (G) – the goal of the initiative
- (R) – the current reality and the relevant considerations surrounding the initiative
- (O) – the number of options
- (W) – a way forward.

In taking this approach you become crystal clear on what your boss wants, they become clear on what your intended course of action is, and these give you the highly desirable outcome that you're both 100% on the same page.

As an added benefit, the process also allows you to demonstrate your ability to think through the scenario and develop an appropriate plan that meets your boss' intentions and goals. This demonstrates your own competence and inspires a greater level of confidence and trust in you. This in turn is likely to result in them providing you a greater level of freedom, autonomy and responsibility as you go about your work.

Scenario 2: Changing a problematic course of action

When considering the problematic course of action scenario, what we're really talking about is changing your boss' mind. It's not uncommon for leaders to make decisions based on strategic intent without considering or being aware of the tactical implications felt by the workers on the ground. And that means that it's equally common for team members to feel that the course of action the leader is suggesting is just not feasible.

In this situation it is both appropriate and advisable for the team members on the ground to try to respectfully challenge the course of action. Of course those team members might find this hard to do. But when there's a culture of coaching, it will certainly be easier. And it's important to try to make them aware of the implications, so they're better able to make a more informed decision.

When it comes to changing your boss' mind, both coaching skills and asking strategic questions are great ways to challenge decisions and raise awareness. When used in the right way, these tactics can help you interact with your boss and even shift their priorities in a way that comes across as both respectful and helpful in these scenarios.

Five suggested tactics

1. *Plan your conversation.* Consider or plan which questions you were going to ask and consider what your leader's response to those questions might be.

2. *Discuss the possible future with no change.* This allows the leader to think through and articulate the problematic outcomes associated with the current course of action.

3. *Ask them to consider an alternate future that results from a different course of action.* You will be able to accomplish this most effectively if you frame it as a contribution to the priorities of the leader.

4. *Brainstorm possible solutions and alternative options together.* This collaborative approach allows your leader to be involved and retain a sense of ownership over the outcome while allowing you to also influence the process.

5. *Act with care.* Above all, with each of the above steps you must always remain respectful. Don't try to overstep your coaching up techniques.

Remember, you can't *change* your leader's mind

Regardless of how bone headed or misguided we think our leaders are, it's important to remember that no matter how good or how right we are, we cannot *change people's mind* – even when we're coaching up. As coach and good friend of mine David Neal regularly reminds me, 'We cannot change someone's mind. All we can do is provide additional information which *might lead them to a different conclusion*'.

While it's a good thing for team members and workers to respectfully influence those that lead them, it's often the case that the senior leaders have more information about the current situation and more experience from past situations. Chances are they can be right even when those they lead think they're wrong.

In these situations challenging senior leaders in the wrong way can make you look like a fool. When you use coaching skills and strategic questions, however, you are not viewed as *disruptively challenging* but instead *collaboratively challenging*. And this difference presents you as simply curious and willing to learn – even when you've missed the mark. Having curiosity and a willingness to learn are both fantastic traits that your leader will be happy to see and nurture in you.

On the other hand, if you *are* right, your leader's trust, confidence and respect for you will be greatly increased. And you'll find that the leader begins to turn to you for input and collaboration more and more often. So, whether you're right or wrong, as long as your techniques are done respectfully, coaching up always has a positive outcome.

Reflection time

1. In what areas could your leadership benefit from coaching up?

2. When would your next opportunity to coach up be?

CHAPTER ELEVEN

Creating coaching leaders

Coaching culture is about everyone having the necessary skills and commitment to coach upwards, sidewards and every-which-way.'
– Heather-Jane Gray

Becoming a coaching leader doesn't just happen. It requires the intentional investment of time, energy and resources – particularly if an organisation is seeking to take a leadership team on this journey. There are four key phases that leaders and teams go through.

- Phase 1: Establish the foundations

- Phase 2: Experience the difference

- Phase 3: Encourage the evolution

- Phase 4: Embed the transformation

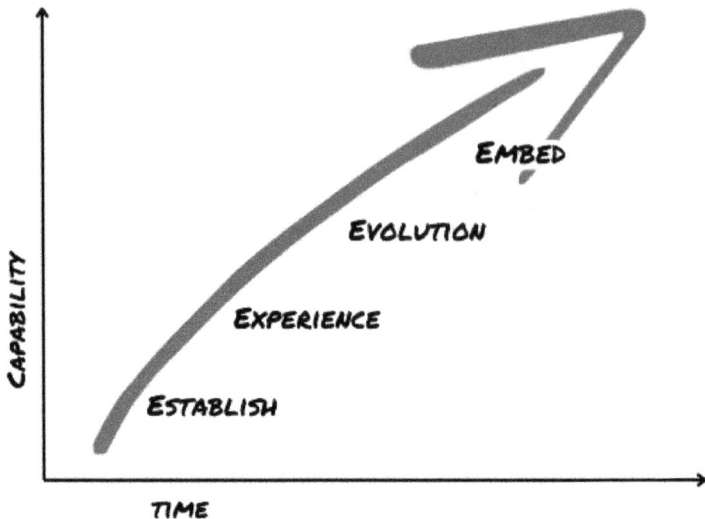

Phase 1: Establish the foundations

Just as with learning any new skill set or becoming a practitioner of any discipline or art form, the first step is training. If you consider the analogy of a pilot, a cadet begins their training in the classroom. They are taught the introductory theory of flight, the basic physics of lift and how the aircraft stays in the air. They are introduced to the instruments in the cockpit and the parts of the aircraft while they are still in the classroom.

We take the same approach when a leader learns to coach. They must first learn exactly what coaching is, understand the process conceptually and consider the outcome they are trying to achieve. They will also need training in coaching skills. While some may think these are everyday conversational skills, the intentionality of how they are used to create a specific effect is not always intuitive.

A past client and I were about to deliver the Coaching Leader Program to the senior leaders of his firm when he made the following statement: 'We've all been around good coaches, good teachers and good leaders. We know it when we see it, but we've never been taught how to do it well.' These leaders were passionate about developing young talent in their business and were taking good steps to do so. However, they recognised they weren't being as effective as they could be in this area.

What they couldn't do with confidence was articulate how they were developing their people and what they needed to do to achieve that outcome. During the first training session of the program, there were a number of light bulb moments for many of the leaders in the room as they began to understand what coaching was, how it differed from their current approach and what they could do differently. At the end of that first training workshop, these leaders were able to clearly articulate the method and approach to coach and develop their people – which meant they could then be intentional about doing so.

Ideally this training is done in a cohort, whether that be as a team or with colleagues from across the organisation. This allows the leaders involved to take the journey towards becoming a coaching leader together. While the formal training provides a shared experience for them to bond around, it also provides a common language with which they can reflect and discuss their experiences.

Sharing is an important element of the learning journey. Again, we're reminded that John Maxwell says, 'Reflection turns experience into insight.'[1] Sharing their insights with colleagues speeds up the development process for both parties and clarifies the leaders' learnings for themselves.

As we've discussed earlier, when we communicate our thoughts, we are forced to articulate them. This act of articulation brings clarity. The more we share our experiences, the clearer our personal insights become.

Taking this journey together provides a safe space for leaders to practise their coaching skills with each other, laying the foundation for informal peer coaching. As leaders are intentional about using a coaching approach to support each other through the training program, they also begin to develop a habit of supporting one another after the formal program concludes. Conducting coaching skills training as a cohort and encouraging supportive coaching-infused interactions throughout the program also helps foster a coaching culture.

The practice of journalling

As a coach and an educator, my focus for those I'm training is the depth and quality of their learning. I want leaders to be able to apply the lessons and insights they learned from me long after the training has ended. I also want those leaders to teach those same lessons to others. But in such a fast-paced world, often the focus for many leaders and organisations is how they can learn these lessons as fast as possible. Luckily there is a practice that not only speeds up the learning journey, but also enhances its depth and quality. That process is journalling.

Journalling has been used for centuries to help people make sense of the world. Journalling allows us to assimilate what we are learning into what we already know, enhancing our understanding of the subject matter and its meaning in the world. It is this assimilation, linking with other pre-existing knowledge banks in our brains, that both deepens and speeds up learning.

Science agrees that writing can help us to learn. Research from Rutgers University found that expressive writing about past experiences – particularly one's failures – increases brain activity (across the dorsal striatum and mid-cingulate cortex, for those interested) in a way that results in significantly greater memory during learning tasks.[2] In other words, when we write about what we are learning, we remember it more.

Journalling can also be described as the process of actively searching for the useful ideas found in our practice. When we write with intent, we are trying to identify and articulate the lessons that can be found in our experience.

As author James Clear writes, 'Almost anything in life can be learned faster. Most people learn passively. They wait for insights to come to them. But you can speed things up by actively searching for useful ideas.'[3]

If we can clearly articulate what works, what doesn't and what we could do more effectively as we learn to use coaching skills, we are more likely to remember them next time we are trying to coach – meaning we are more likely to be intentional about implementing them as we move forward.

Additionally, having a written record of our journey and the lessons learned along the way makes it much easier for leaders to teach those they lead, passing their lessons and learnings on to others, thereby fulfilling the responsibility leaders have to develop capability and produce more leaders.

Phase 2: Experience the difference

Training and instruction in a certain skill is only the first part of the learning journey. To return to the pilot analogy, once the initial classroom instruction has taken place, the cadet must gain experience flying the aircraft. First, they must experience the aircraft in flight, flown by their instructor. Then they must gain experience flying the aircraft themselves, applying the skills and knowledge they were taught on the ground.

Remember when I learned to glide? My instructor Gerhart had control for our first flight in the glider. He demonstrated how to control the glider, and how it should feel when it's going right, or how you might handle it when things go wrong. It wasn't until I had experienced how each of these felt, that I was able to take the controls myself.

In the same way, a leader learning to coach needs to gain the experience of coaching. First, they must experience what it is like being coached. Just as Gerhart had to demonstrate what good gliding looked and felt like, it is important for leaders to understand what good coaching looks like and what it feels like to be coached. There is no better way to do this than being coached yourself.

The experience of being coached

A leader should never ask or expect their staff to do something they are not willing to do themselves. If they are expecting to coach their people, they need to be willing to be coached themselves. To fail to do so, fails to embrace the key belief of 'me first' that is characteristic of the coaching leader's mindset.

The reality is that being coached is often a difficult experience. Giving answers is easy. It is easy for the leader and for the student. It allows them to remain passive and get by with minimal thinking. Part of being coached is being challenged and prompted to do the hard thinking – the thinking that one wouldn't normally engage in if they were not being coached.

Doing the hard thinking *is* hard. It can be uncomfortable. It can be frustrating. At the same time, the feeling of satisfaction and fulfilment one gains from the insights discovered and the a-ha moments that occur during coaching can be truly exciting and motivating. Experiencing the breadth of these emotions is important for leaders, as it allows them to relate to and empathise with their people during the coaching process.

Often the key to both successful coaching and navigating the coaching process is being able to adopt the right perspective towards both the focus of the coaching but also the coaching process. 'Perspective,' Brené Brown says, 'is the function of experience. The less experience we have, the less perspective you can take.'[4] If, as coaching leaders, we want to help our people adopt a beneficial perspective towards coaching, we need to have experience in doing so ourselves.

It's also important for the leader to learn what different and difficult coaching scenarios feel like and how an experienced coach handles them. I remember feeling the glider begin to stall and noting how Gerhart would respond, remaining calm but immediately pushing forward on the stick or rolling the aircraft to pick up airspeed again.

It is also possible for a coaching session to stall, where a leader and the individual being coached don't know what to do or where to go next. In such scenarios, a leader must remain calm and change tact, employ a different coaching technique or, when appropriate, shift away from coaching into a different leadership approach. The best way for a leader to learn how to do this is to experience what a stalled coaching session feels like and observe how an experienced coach handles the situation.

Ideally, this initial coaching experience for leaders learning to coach should be conducted by someone with significant experience. They do not need to be a professional executive coach. They simply have to be experienced and have enough mastery of coaching skills and the coaching process to be able to teach and develop the skill set in others. However, for organisations that are only just introducing coaching and have not had a culture of coaching in the past, often the best option is to engage an external coach.

It is also important that coaching during this stage is balanced. It should include coaching leaders to coach, to intentionally apply the coaching skills they are learning and to facilitate the reflection process to both speed up and enhance the development of the leader's coaching capability. However, it should not be solely focused on coaching others.

The journey to becoming a coaching leader doesn't result in being a professional executive coach. The coaching leader is a leader, first and foremost. This coaching should also have a focus on developing their overall general leadership abilities and their leadership practice – not just their coaching abilities. Again, if leaders are going to coach their people to be better leaders, they need the experience of being coached to be better leaders – not just better coaches.

There is another aspect of this initial coaching experience for leaders learning to coach that may differ from other coaching experiences. That is, that the coach should be transparent with the leader in the skills, techniques and approaches they are using. If the coach or leader doing the coaching is explicitly explaining their approach and decision to use it before, during and/or after employing the technique, the leader being coached is able to first, engage with that approach more intentionally and second, understand how and why different techniques are used, the impacts they might have and the insights they may generate.

The experience of coaching

Of course the experience stage of a coaching leader's development is not just about gaining experience of being coached, but also about gaining experience coaching and applying coaching skills to lead. While formal training is necessary and important, particularly if one is new to coaching, the opportunity to apply these new skills is where the real learning occurs.

A study carried out by Dr Salott Chau of the Macau University of Science and Technology and Dr Catherine Cheung of Hong Kong Polytechnic University identified a positive relationship between active learning – which connects students to the real-life situations they will encounter in their future jobs – and student engagement that is reflected in the components of practical skills enhancement.[5] The one substantially enhances the other.

> *'Learning is defined by taking action. You haven't learned a thing until you can take action and use it.'*
> – Ken Blanchard

As the leader gains experience using coaching skills, they have the opportunity to experiment. Which coaching skills work in which scenarios? Which coaching skills come naturally, and which need more preparation, intentional practice and development? As the leader continues to gain experience through experimentation, they will have successes and be buoyed by the results they achieve when their coaching approach works and bears fruit.

They are also bound to make mistakes. And it's important that they do because mistakes are often where we find our greatest learning. As B.J. Neblett said, 'Experience is the sum total of all the mistakes we have made in life.'

Learning to approach mistakes, both their own and those of their people, with a sense of curiosity and determination is part of a coaching leader's developmental journey. They should employ curiosity to uncover why something didn't work in the situation and determination to identify the insight to be learned and applied in the future. Often it is the discipline of journalling that helps a leader conduct this exploration and process the mistake to harness its value.

Another aspect of experimentation involves discovering which aspects of their leadership roles best suit taking a coaching approach. Leaders will need to be mindful of their current role and the context within which they lead. For example, the way a frontline leader uses coaching skills may be very different to the way a senior executive does.

Frontline leaders (whether they have a title and position or not) may be less likely to have opportunities for formal one-on-one coaching and it may be inappropriate for them to overtly coach those around them. Instead, they may need to rely on using coaching skills informally. It may be inserting a question or two into the daily stand-up or asking a team member to clarify the purpose of a task before initiating. Gently using reframing to encourage colleagues to stay positive or simply asking what they could do differently over lunch still constitutes.

Senior leaders, however, will have more easily recognisable opportunities to coach. As they conduct meetings, facilitate planning sessions, hold performance reviews and lead projects, they are presented with a myriad of opportunities to apply coaching skills. Remember that everything a leader does is an opportunity to develop people if they are intentional about doing so.

Almost any task a leader does, by themselves or with others, can be enhanced by using coaching skills. The more experience one gains, the more comfortable and confident they become employing a coaching approach as part of their leadership style. It is really in the application of coaching skills as one leads that a leader not only practises their coaching, but also develops their leadership practice.

Phase 3: Encourage the evolution

The more experience a leader has, the more confident they will be in a given situation. Confidence, however, does not always translate into growth or improvement. Nor does experience and confidence equate to the development of leadership identity – who the leader is, as opposed to what skills they possess. For this to occur, there needs to be an intentional pursuit of improvement and development.

Once a cadet is trained and receives his wings, licensed to fly by himself or perhaps with others, he can officially be called a pilot. Does that mean they *are* a pilot? Or are they simply an individual who is licensed to pilot an aircraft?

It is only through continued experience, a multitude of flight hours and additional training that an individual begins to automatically think like a pilot, behave like a pilot and react like a pilot. It is at this point, when they react to situations without having to make conscious decisions to engage their training, that they have truly *become* a pilot. 'Pilot' is no longer a persona or a role they step into, it is who they are.

For the pilot, this evolution was not one that started as a cadet and finished with their flight training. The journey is one that continued over time. It involved more advanced training, new skills such as instrument ratings, night flying or aerobatics training. It is likely to have involved conversion training or a type rating to fly different size aircraft. At some point it would involve flying to, in and through different locations, environments and weather conditions. This provides the opportunity for the pilot to apply their skills in a range of different scenarios. The more experience and, importantly, the wider or greater breadth of experience over time, the more the evolution from becoming a pilot to *being* a pilot takes place.

The same is true of leaders. The sad reality is that most leaders have not had quality leadership training or been provided with a breadth of experience to apply what skills they have. They remain individuals who occupy leadership roles and many fail to make the real transformation to become leaders.

The journey to becoming a coaching leader is no different. For the majority of leaders who are trained in the use of coaching skills, they may pick up a few skills they apply as they move forward in their leadership role. Yet they remain leaders who can coach, rather than making the transition to really becoming coaching leaders.

It is only with the continued intentional application over time, in different scenarios and across a variety of environments, that leaders develop their coaching mindset, skill set and practice in a way that allows them to evolve into coaching leaders.

What are you happy with?

The reality is that for many who learn to fly, they have no intention of becoming a Top Gun graduate or an airline captain. They may be happy being a lawyer, engineer, doctor or farmer who has the ability to experience the thrill of flying once a month or on the weekend. It's important to note that this is completely OK.

The same is true in the world of leadership. There will be some leaders who will read this book, be totally inspired to lead in a way that develops others and decide to commit to the evolutionary journey of becoming a coaching leader. There will be others who are happy with their current leadership approach and are simply interested in picking up one or two new skills that might make them more effective.

That is completely OK, as long as you are making the conscious choice about which one you choose. I would hate for you to desire one option but end up realising the other, ending your leadership journey unfulfilled and with regret.

Pursue the evolution

The key to pursuing this evolution is intentionality. It requires intentionality to maintain the discipline to continually identify the opportunities to apply coaching skills and actually do it. As John Maxwell writes, 'Motivation may get you going, but discipline keeps you growing.'[6] You may end your coaching training feeling highly motivated to continue, but unless you are intentional and disciplined about continuing to practise and develop your skill set, your journey will stop short. Your potential will be unrealised.

This intentional discipline may take many forms and will look different for everyone. It may be planning ahead and looking at your schedule on a daily or weekly basis to identify opportunities to coach. It may involve being conscious of using coaching skills in meetings, in one-on-one sessions or performance reviews. It will likely include deliberately looking for opportunities to apply skills in new ways and in different scenarios.

One of the best disciplines to help cultivate this sense of intentionality and encourage evolution is that of journalling. Once again, the deliberate approach to reviewing, reflecting, and articulating insights and lessons is critical before one can plan how to apply those insights and improve moving forward.

As well as being intentional and disciplined about applying and improving their initial skill set, leaders who are cultivating coaching leadership are also continuing to add to their skill set and understanding. Just as a pilot receives additional training to be able to fly at night or by instruments, leaders should also seek out additional coaching training, whether that be formal accreditation or masterclasses.

There are a myriad of online courses available, online webinars, lectures and tutorials that could help. And of course, there are plenty of books on coaching and leadership which will also assist. Adding to the skill set, whether that be through new techniques, new models or a greater understanding of the psychology of people, is an important part of the continuing evolution.

You will notice I have used the word intentional a lot in this section of the book.

A word for senior leaders

If you are a senior leader who is sponsoring a coaching program among your leaders and desire the coaching approach to be central to the way your team leads, there are a couple things you can do to encourage your team to continue the evolution.

1. **Lead from the front.** This is about embodying the 'me first' principle that is characteristic of the coaching leader mindset. If you want your people to understand that coaching is important to you as the leader, you need to demonstrate it by adopting a coaching approach with them. Role model the behaviour you want them to adopt with their teams.

2. **Keep it front of mind.** This means talking about coaching regularly. It can be easy to be sucked back into the vortex of work and just to keep pace by reverting to the old, quick and easy behaviours of telling. Keep coaching front of mind by sharing your experiences of coaching, new skills you might be learning or articles you've read or videos you've watched about coaching. You might use coaching skills in a meeting and then at the end highlight that that's what you were doing.

3. **Keep them accountable.** In your one-on-one meetings or conversations with individuals in your team, ask them about their plans to apply coaching and then check in on their progress at a later time. Simply having the conversation regularly with them will communicate that developing their coaching capability is a priority for you as their leader and will keep them informally accountable.

One step at a time

The key to successfully evolving is consistency over time. The journey to becoming a coaching leader is an evolution, not a revolution. Making significantly revolutionary changes can be hard to maintain as a leader and manage as a team member. However, small changes and small improvements consistently made over time produce significant results over the long term. This is the principle of the aggregation of marginal gains.

As coach John Wooden said:

When you improve a little each day, eventually big things occur... Don't look for the quick, big improvement. Seek the small improvement one day at a time. That's the only way it happens – and when it happens, it lasts.

Phase 4: Embed the transformation

While gaining experience and continuing the evolution are focused on discovery, development and learning, the final stage of this journey is embedding. Embedding learning is as much about embodying a new identity as it is about changing behaviour. It is about developing habits so that the behaviours characteristic of the new identity become ingrained. Just as the pilot seeks to make conducting ground checks, using checklists and regularly scanning the sky habitual, so a coaching leader seeks to make adopting a coaching approach habitual.

When it comes to building the habits required to become a coaching leader, I recommend beginning with Michael Bungay Stanier's three-step process. In his book, *The Coaching Habit*, he outlines the following three steps:

1. Identify the trigger: 'When this happens…'
2. Identify the old behaviour: 'Instead of…'
3. Identify the new behaviour: 'I will…'[7]

This process forces a leader to clearly articulate the when, what and how of their habit, allowing them to set their intention, make their commitment and be intentional about ingraining the new behaviour.

Once these habits have been built, they will begin to influence the way the leader leads. They will result in changes to the informal or personal processes the leader uses when approaching various situations in their day-to-day leadership. These changes are the evidence that real learning has taken place.

As Zenger and Folkman write in *The Extraordinary Leader*, 'Real learning results in new behaviour.'[8] And it is likely this new behaviour will be noticed by others. Remember the story of the two sergeants? Their personnel noticed the changes and asked about them. This presented the opportunity for the sergeants to share with their people the journey they were on and teach them some of the coaching skills.

As the philosopher and essayist Joseph Joubert once wrote, 'To teach is to learn twice over.'[9] Robert Heinlein, author, engineer and naval officer, expressed the same sentiment when he said, 'When one teaches, two learn.'

When a leader teaches what they have learned, they are not only articulating the learning, which brings additional clarity for the leader, but also forces them to think about how they would express that learning in a way that best resonates with their people. This thinking differently about the subject deepens the learning and encodes it in a different way within their brain. Thus the learning is embedded further for the leader.

Teaching others also has the additional benefit of socialising the concept of coaching with the leader's team. It makes coaching an explicit process that becomes normalised across the team, paving the way for team members to not only engage in the coaching delivered by the leader, but also encouraging them to adopt coaching behaviours in their own work and with each other. In this way, coaching becomes embedded not just in the psyche and behaviour of the leader, but also within the culture of the organisation.

CHAPTER TWELVE

Creating a coaching culture

'A coaching culture starts with the leader's willingness to engage in the coaching relationship and to undertake reflection, to develop themselves and others.'
– Sattar Bawany

If an organisation is investing time and money to equip their leaders with coaching skills and encourage them to become coaching leaders, they likely want coaching to become part of the workplace culture. The embedding of coaching behaviours, not just in leaders but into organisational culture, creates a 'coaching culture'.

In his book, *The Heart of Coaching*, Thomas Crane describes a coaching culture being present when, '[A]ll members of the culture fearlessly engage in candid, respectful coaching conversations, unrestricted by reporting relationships, about how they can improve their working relationships and individual and collective work performance.'[1] A coaching culture is not just dependent on the presence of formal coaching, but occurs when staff support each other using coaching skills and techniques in everyday interactions.

The major elements that assist in the creation of a coaching culture are articulated below. There are strategic elements that link to and are included in some of the formal structural elements of the organisation that influence culture, then there are the operational opportunities to promote coaching. All of these operate within the context of informal behaviour demonstrated by staff as they go about their day-to-day work.

Starting with the more strategic elements and moving towards the more operational ones, let's look at each element more closely.

Alignment with values

Values help articulate the identity of the organisation – who it is and how it operates. Values describe the key characteristics of the desired culture. For coaching to be successfully embedded in an organisation's culture, there should be an alignment between the values of an organisation and the principles of coaching. One way to evaluate this is to look at the key beliefs that characterise a coaching leader's mindset.

For employees to really embrace coaching and for it to be deliberately made part of the culture, people need to see how coaching contributes to the organisation. Many companies have statements that describe how values influence behaviour or what living out particular values looks like in day-to-day business. To formalise the desire to create a coaching culture, such statements should include descriptions of how coaching may be used as a mechanism for living out particular values.

Psychologist Susan David writes that 'values without action are just aspirations'.[2] Articulating coaching as an action for employees to take not only helps staff live out the values and create the culture the organisation desires, but also helps them engage in coaching.

Inclusion in the organisational strategy

The strategy of an organisation informs its priorities, and those of its leaders. It is from strategy that goals, objectives and KPIs are developed, and against which performance is measured. Leaders will pursue what is important to their leaders and the organisation, what they are held accountable to and what they are rewarded for. They are unlikely to invest time, energy and resources into what is not prioritised by the organisation.

As Jack Welch once said, 'Strategy is simply resource allocation.' So if we want our leaders to invest their limited resources into developing a coaching culture, we need to include coaching in the workforce strategy of the organisation.

In recent years, the Royal Australian Air Force has done just this. Its Air Force Strategy 2017–2027 included a People Capability Vector that sought to create an 'agile, innovative workforce'.[3] Alongside this strategic direction was Plan Jericho, a long-term series of initiatives designed to transform the organisation into a fifth-generation Air Force. Coaching is articulated as one of the mechanisms by which a fifth-generation people capability was developed.

One of the Plan Jericho initiatives was the Air Force Leadership Coaching Program (AFLCP). These initiatives have carried through to the latest *Air Force Strategy (AFSTRAT) 2020* document that describes Line of Effort 2: Developing an intelligent and skilled workforce.[4] Plan Jericho and the AFLCP continue to be an active part of the organisational strategy.

Organisational artefacts

Artefacts are those things you see as you walk through a workplace that provide the physical evidence of the culture. This physical evidence will emerge over time to reflect the culture that is at play. Organisational leaders can also use artefacts to influence culture. The reality is that you cannot force culture on people (without being authoritarian and creating a toxic culture). You can, however, create an environment that fosters the culture you desire.

Artefacts can influence culture in two main ways. First, they can act as a visual cue. Objects like posters, dashboards and quotes displayed in a prominent location can remind people of cultural priorities. For example, many of my clients display posters of coaching models in their workplaces. This keeps coaching front of mind for the leaders, prompting them to ask a question rather than give advice during meetings or to self-coach as they prepare for a difficult conversation.

Second, artefacts can also more directly shape behaviour. One organisation I have been involved with completely redesigned the forms they used for performance reviews to facilitate leaders and managers adopting a coaching approach with their people. There were boxes for goals and action plans to be articulated. It was expected that for each goal articulated, leaders would have mini GROW conversations with their staff.

Designing and distributing coaching-inspired artefacts throughout the workplace alone is not sufficient to create a coaching culture. Culture change still requires commitment from leaders. However, creating the right artefacts does help shape the environment in a way that makes the transition towards a coaching culture easier for both leaders and staff.

Policy and procedures

Most organisations use policy and procedures as a mechanism to translate strategy into operations. Formally incorporating coaching into policy and procedures documents is another way to shape the behaviour of leaders. This can be a more overt form of influence requiring a level of compliance from leaders and can be a mechanism that enables senior leaders to hold their people accountable to employing coaching approaches.

One example might be that a performance management policy might stipulate that the individual in question should be coached by their manager in parallel or as part of the performance management process. Additionally, often procedures are linked to organisational artefacts. In the organisation that redesigned their performance review templates, the accompanying procedure specifically described using a coaching approach to conduct the performance review.

Again, it should be noted that leaders should never rely on policy and procedures to enforce a coaching culture. This is a complementary measure that helps create an environment that fosters coaching as a key element of the workplace culture.

Formal coaching and mentoring programs

While a coaching culture manifests when informal coaching is occurring in everyday behaviour, formal coaching still has a significant place for the development of individual capability and normalising coaching within the workplace.

The formal opportunities for coaching can take a number of different forms. The most common is **individual coaching**. While leaders will have the opportunity to coach those they lead, most formal coaching is conducted with an external coach. These individual coaching sessions may be initiated with a focus on a specific developmental need or workplace challenge. They can often be attached to organisational leadership programs, providing leaders with the opportunity to discuss and explore the application of the program content to the specific context of the individual leader.

Another form these programs can take is that of **internal mentoring arrangements**, often being cross-departmental in nature. In addition to providing the opportunity for leaders to be coached, these arrangements can also provide cross-pollination of ideas and break down silos within organisations.

One type of coaching that is becoming more common is that of **team coaching**. Predominantly conducted by a coach/leader external to the team, the coaching is focused at the team level. The team-coach facilitates the discussion amongst the team to solve collective challenges, facilitate more effective collaboration and cohesion, and ultimately to increase team performance.

Finally, another form of coaching that helps build a coaching culture is **formalised peer coaching.** Peer coaching circles are a cost-effective initiative that provides a space for leaders to practise their coaching skills, as well as support their peers in an intentional way.

Coaching skills training

Heather-Jane Gray, founder of a global leadership development and coaching company, says a 'coaching culture is about everyone having the necessary skills and commitment to coach upwards, sideways and every which way'. If we want everyone to be using coaching across the workplace, we need to give them the skills necessary to do so. As such, coaching skills training is an important part of establishing a coaching culture.

There are a number of different options for such training. There is the formal accreditation option, where the training is provided by a registered training organisation and (here in Australia) resulting in either a Cert IV or Diploma level qualification, or accreditation by a global peak body such as the International Coaching Federation (ICF).

This training is usually the first step for those wanting to become executive coaches and is therefore comprehensive. While such comprehensive training provides leaders with an excellent skill set, it is not always practical for many organisations.

A popular option is to have an external practitioner provide coaching skills training to leaders. Such training is often more cost-effective and can be tailored to the organisation's needs. There is also the option to have internal staff deliver training. For this to be successful, however, the organisation has to have the right people who have the right skills and experience, and importantly are passionate about coaching.

Too often in an effort to save money, I have seen internal training delivered by individuals who provide a poor experience for staff. This poor experience – particularly if it's their first exposure to coaching – actually turns staff off coaching altogether and does more to undermine a coaching culture than to build it.

The final consideration about coaching skills training within an organisation is to what level it will be conducted. Many organisations that provide coaching training do so to their leaders. However, there is significant merit to providing some level of training to all staff across the organisation. If we want our staff at all levels to show more initiative, solve their own problems, be more innovative and support each other using a coaching approach, then explicitly equipping them with the skills to do so is the fastest way to that end state.

Depending on the size of the organisation, any combination of these training options could be used. The Air Force Leadership Coaching Program uses all of them. Each year, it sends a number of its leaders away to conduct formal accredited training. These leaders then not only have the ability to provide individual coaching across the country, they also run internal coaching skills training to groups at all levels of the organisation. Coaching skills training has also been integrated into recruit training, officer training and many of the other employment training units, meaning the majority of Air Force personnel are exposed to coaching skills training at multiple points throughout their career.

Skills training is not just an important part of establishing a coaching culture, but also maintaining it. Whether or not the organisation seeks to train all staff or just those in leadership roles, provision will need to be made for training new people entering the company or being promoted. Periodic refresher or advanced training may also be used to encourage the evolution of those previously trained.

Whatever it looks like in an organisation, coaching skills training should never be a 'once and done' thing if coaching is to become and remain part of the company culture.

Informal coaching behaviours

In any organisation, the behaviours of its people are often the best evidence of its culture. It is there we must look to measure the progress of establishing a coaching culture. Regardless of the number or quality of the formal initiatives an organisation puts in place to influence its culture, it is the everyday behaviour of its people that has the greatest influence on, and ultimately is, the company culture.

Natalie Ashdown, in her book *Bring Out Their Best*, explains a coaching culture in a simple equation:

The way we do things around here + coaching
= coaching culture[5]

What does that look like? Natalie describes it in the following way: 'When it is a person's preference to use coaching skills, to ask questions rather than giving solutions, to hold back and listen, and prefer to coach and grow people rather than simply make them do what you want – that's when you have a coaching culture in place.'[6]

The aim is for coaching to be part of the informal everyday behaviours of the workforce – for coaching to simply be the way we do things around here. It takes time and intentionality from leaders who must embrace and role model coaching. It takes ongoing investment and reinforcement. It takes time for skills to be developed, experience to be gained and learning to be embedded.

Eventually, a coaching culture begins to take hold. Then the stage is set. The environment is created for not only individuals to unlock new levels of performance at work, but the entire organisation to realise its full potential as well.

Reflection Time:

1. What coaching behaviours would you like to see become part of the culture in your workplace?

2. What needs to happen to achieve that?

3. What could *you* do to make that a reality?

CHAPTER THIRTEEN

Coaching beyond the workplace

'A good coach can change a game.
A great coach can change a life.'
– John Wooden

Once a leader is on the journey to becoming a coaching leader, coaching gradually becomes part of who they are – both as a leader in the workplace and as a person outside of work. Coaching conversations won't be limited to during work hours.

Leaders will find coaching creeping into their interactions outside of work, whether it be with a friend going through a challenging time, coaching their daughter's soccer team or navigating a family conflict. Once a leader understands the benefits of coaching, possesses a coaching skill set and has experience using it, they will find themselves using that skill set with others across many areas of their life.

Improve yourself

As John Maxwell says, 'The only way to improve your life is to improve yourself.'[1] If we as leaders have developed a skill set to grow and improve others, we are remiss if we don't use that same skill set to improve ourselves and our own lives.

I encourage you to sit down and think about the most important areas of your life. Assess your effectiveness in each, and then set goals and develop plans to improve in each of these areas.

I like to use the 5F model I picked up from my first business coach, Wez Hone.

The 5F model

The 5Fs are:

- Faith

- Family

- Finance

- Fitness

- Fun

Every year, I sit down and set goals in each of these five areas and coach myself to improve my life. While the model below is built around the 5Fs, if you simply google 'Wheel of life', a myriad of variations will appear that include different options for the areas of life you would like to work on. I encourage you to find one that resonates with you.

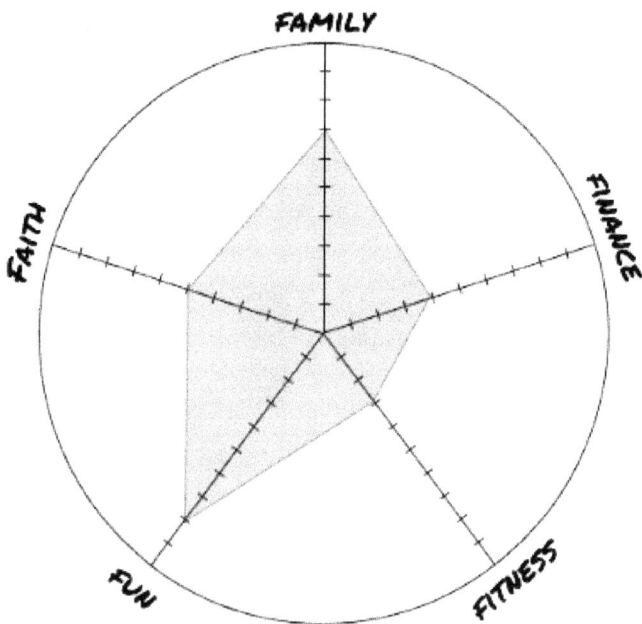

How to use the 5F model

On a scale of 1-10, assess where you are and circle the relevant mark on each of the 5Fs. This provides a visual representation of how balanced your life and where you might want to be more intentional. Decide where you want to be on each vector and set one or two goals for each and coach yourself to a better life.

The importance of setting and achieving goals outside of work cannot be understated. Modern science on work-life balance and wellbeing revolves around the concept of how we recover from our work. As any elite athlete will tell you, the secret to high performance is getting the right balance between training/performance and recovery. Elite athletes can become fanatical about their recovery because they know if they don't get enough, they will not be able to perform. The same principle applies to our work. If we want to perform at the highest levels possible in our work, we need to make sure we get the necessary recovery.

The latest research in this area suggests that three key activities are required to recover from work: detachment, relaxation and mastery.[2] It is the last one I wish to focus on here. Mastery is all about setting and achieving recreational goals. These could be physical goals such as running a marathon, developing a skill set such as learning a new language or undertaking a project such as writing a book.

The act of setting and achieving goals is important for several reasons. First, it requires us to focus on achieving our goals and encourages us to detach from work, which is one of the other keys to effective recovery. Second, it gives us a sense of progress and control, boosting our sense of self-efficacy.

This is particularly important for leaders who are experiencing high workloads and challenging work environments where they often feel like they aren't making any progress at work. The psychological benefits of achievement in one area of life often carry over into other areas. The sense of progress one gets from achieving outside of work can be encouraging, even inspiring, when one steps back into the workplace. If I can run a marathon (or insert any significant achievement), I can deal with this workload (or whatever the workplace challenge).

Experienced coaching leaders don't just limit their coaching to the workplace, they are also intentional about coaching themselves outside of work. They know that doing so not only makes for a better, more enjoyable life, but also helps facilitate the necessary recovery so they can personally sustain higher performance once they step back into the workplace.

Coaching leadership at home

If you stop and think about what a leader is trying to achieve when coaching their staff, is that not also what any parent wants for their children? A leader coaches their people to develop them, make them more proactive and possess more motivation and initiative, help them to learn and become great problem solvers, and to be high performers who work to achieve their goals. These are all things we want for our kids. It makes sense then, that if we as leaders have a skill set that facilitates these qualities and outcomes, that we would also use it to help those most important to us.

Using coaching skills with our kids is not only a safe place to practise – there are very few lasting consequences if we get it wrong – it's also a great way to foster their development and independence as they grow.

Consider an example of my youngest daughter asking me to turn the light on for her. I saw the opportunity and took it. I responded with, 'What would you do if Dad wasn't here?' She looked at me and thought for a moment, then walked over to the wall near the switch. She wedged her toe on top of the cornice and nimbly stepped up long enough to reach up and turn on the light. Her smile as she turned, realising she had just done something she had never done before was priceless.

I try to use coaching as much as I can in my parenting. It has helped me to develop empathy in my eldest as she navigates playground politics with her friends. It has helped me to foster an understanding in my daughters of how their choices impact others. It has also helped me to nurture a growth mindset in them and a sense of self-belief that they can achieve whatever they set their mind to.

The impact of a coaching approach to parenting only increases as children get older. Many of my former students have told me about the positive outcomes they experienced from using these skills on their children. There are two cases that stand out.

Both were fathers, one in the military and the other a corrections officer. Both were hard men who were having significant troubles with their sons. In both cases, they shared their amazement as they described the 'breakthrough' they had when they adopted a coaching approach. One even had tears in his eyes as he spoke of achieving a level of connection with his son he had not felt in years. Such is the power of asking rather than telling.

A word of caution

Before you jump into coaching around the home, let me share two pieces of advice. I learned these lessons the hard way and I'm sharing so you don't have to.

1. **Don't start too young.** Coaching requires a level of cognitive development and life experience to be effective. One of the biggest mistakes many parents (especially me) make is expecting too much of their kids when their brains are still developing.

   Trying to coach your kids when they aren't ready for it only exasperates them, and *you*. The right time to start will be different for each child. I can successfully coach my four year old on some things, but not on others. At the same time, I know I can't take the same approach to my nephew of the same age. And that's OK. He's just not developmentally ready yet.

Know your kids, experiment, but don't persist if they are too young. By the time they are six, you should be pretty safe to start coaching the simple stuff.

2. **Don't try to coach your spouse.** Especially if they are a trained coach (like mine is). For most people, the relationship with their life partner is a space where they seek safety, comfort and support, particularly when they are facing stressful scenarios both in and out of work.

   At the end of the day when they come home and share their troubles, they want to feel heard and understood, not challenged and pushed outside their comfort zone. Unless they specifically ask you for it, don't try to coach them. If they want a coach, a mentor or a therapist, they will go and find one.

A better world

I'm passionate about coaching because it is a practice, a discipline and a mechanism by which leaders can truly transform the lives of the people they lead. I've worked with many leaders in my time. I've worked for some of the best of leaders – those whom I would gladly follow into battle and take a bullet for. I have also worked under some of the worst of leaders and have seen the destruction that poor leaders wreak.

Poor leaders can destroy individuals, teams, organisations and even entire countries. Sadly, those individuals exposed to too much poor leadership for too long, too often go home and destroy the lives of their spouse, their kids and their families.

I've also witnessed the great power of truly transformational leaders. They lead in a way that transforms their people into better versions of themselves. These better people are better workers and leaders in their own right. They make up better and higher performing teams, which result in better, more successful organisations. More successful organisations leads to a better economy, which is great for the nation.

But, more importantly, those better people go home and are better husbands and fathers, better mothers and wives, better brothers and sisters, uncles, aunts, nephews and nieces. Better husbands, wives, fathers and mothers leads to better families, which means better, healthier communities and ultimately a better world.

Arguably the world's best sporting coach of all time, John Wooden, said, 'A good coach can change a game. A great coach can change a life.'

I would add that that changed life could go on to change many more lives, each one changing many more lives. Some will be mothers and fathers. Some may be presidents, CEOs and world leaders. In that way, a great coach can change the world. It may sound lofty and altruistic, but I know it to be true. I've seen it and experienced it. You can too.

A call to purpose

When I was growing up, I was in the Boys' Brigade. Established in 1883, it is the oldest youth organisation in the world. Unlike other youth organisations such as Scouts, Boys' Brigade has a formal rank structure. Promotion was not a matter of completing tasks and achievement badges. It was based on character and leadership potential.

As boys, we were taught that the highest honour we could gain was to be promoted, as it was evidence of the quality of young men we were becoming. I reminded myself of this every time I was promoted, both within the Brigade and later in the military.

As an experienced leader, I have come to learn that there is a greater honour than being promoted: that is seeing my people promoted. My proudest moments have been seeing those I have led grow, develop and succeed. Many have gone on to achieve more than I ever did in the particular area or industry we worked together. I consider it to be one of the greatest honours to know I have played a part in not only their success, but in their development as a human being.

Consider the example of an airline captain who, after 40 years of flying and upon retirement, could choose to look at his contribution in several different ways. He could determine the number of passengers he had helped by safely delivering them from one destination to the next. Or he could calculate each fare to determine how much total revenue he had generated for the company.

Alternatively, he could consider the contribution he made to the development of capability to the airline. How many pilots became better pilots as a result of flying with him? Let's say he contributed to the development of 50 other captains throughout his career (though the number is likely to be much higher). Now let's consider the total number of passengers those 50 captains have safely transported and the revenue each one has generated across their careers. The numbers are exponentially higher. The contribution and impact is exponentially greater. And what if we consider the capability development provided by each of those 50 captains? The contribution continues to grow exponentially.

'If you want to awaken all of humanity, then awaken all of yourself. If you want to remove suffering in the world, then remove all that is dark and negative with you. Truly the greatest gift you have to give is that of your own self-transformation.'
– Lao Tzu

As I draw this book to a close, I want to invite you on a journey. It's a journey that will have its ups and downs, its twists and turns. It will be a long journey and it will be difficult at times. It is a journey that requires intentional investment of energy, effort and resources. There will be sacrifices and few immediate rewards.

And yet, there will be times along the way and in the end when you will realise it was a journey worth taking – when you see the results and are filled with the satisfaction that comes from knowing you've helped improve people's performance at work and the fulfilment of knowing you've made people's lives better.

The journey to becoming a coaching leader is truly a transformative one. Yes, you are part of transforming those you lead into better versions of themselves. However, in becoming a coaching leader, you also transform yourself into a better leader and a better version of yourself. And that truly is the greatest gift you have to give.

Final reflection

1. Where would you gain the most value if you applied coaching leadership outside the workplace?

2. What has been the most valuable insight you've gained by reading this book?

3. What are you going to do to implement that insight?

An invitation

Hopefully by now you've realised I'm passionate about how coaching can improve your leadership and your life. I love being part of people experiencing insight that has a significant impact. While I can't see the light bulb go on or hear the penny drop like I might if I was in a coaching session with you, I would still very much like to be part of your experience. I'd love it if you would be willing to share your insights with me. Even better, I'd love to hear about any big wins, significant successes or beneficial breakthroughs you might have by implementing the concepts in this book.

I invite you to send your insights and stories through to
insights@lumian.com.au

It would be greatly appreciated.

Endnotes

Chapter 1

1. Rohn, J. (2019). [Tweet]. SUCCESS magazine [@ successmagazine],Twitter. Accessed at https://twitter.com/ successmagazine/status/1085997755770826752.

2. PwC. (2013). Millennials at work – Reshaping the workplace. Accessed at https://www.pwc.com/co/es/publicaciones/assets/ millennials-at-work.pdf.

3. Hamer, B. Why attracting and retaining the top Millennial talent is key to future success. PwC. Accessed at https://www.pwc.com.au/ digitalpulse/millennials-five-generations-workplace.html

4. Willyerd, K. (2015). Millennials Want to Be Coached at Work. Harvard Business Review. Accessed at https://hbr.org/2015/02/ millennials-want-to-be-coached-at-work.

5. Zenger, J. (2012). We Wait Too Long to Train Our Leaders. Harvard Business Review. Accessed at https://hbr.org/2012/12/why-do-we- wait-so-long-to-trai.

6. Baker, M (2019). Gartner Says 45% of Managers Lack Confidence To Help Employees Develop the Skills They Need Today. Gartner. Accessed at https://www.gartner.com/en/newsroom/ press-releases/2019-09-18-gartner-says-45--of-managers-lack- confidence-to-help-.

7. Ranadive, A. (2018). Ask vs. Tell. Medium. Accessed at https:// medium.com/@ameet/ask-vs-tell-d3e9343d7aeb.

8. Hall, C. (2015). The Coaching Mindset: 8 Ways to Think Like a Coach. [EBook]

Chapter 2

1. Eversfield, C. (2015). The godfather of modern coaching! LinkedIn Pulse. Accessed at https://www.linkedin.com/pulse/godfather-modern-coaching-chris-eversfield/.

2. Gallwey, W.T. (2015). The Inner Game of Tennis: The classic guide to the mental side of peak performance. Pan.

3. Berry, I. (2017). Coaching: Ask Better Questions, Become A Better Coach. CreateSpace Independent Publishing Platform.

4. Whitmore, J. (2002). Coaching for performance: GROWing people, performance and purpose: The principles and practices of coaching and leadership. (3rd ed.). Nicholas Brealey.

5. Lopez-Garrido, G. (2020). Self-Efficacy Theory. Simply Psychology. https://www.simplypsychology.org/self-efficacy.html

6. Ryan, R.M. and Deci, E.L. (2000). Self-Determination Theory and the Facilitation of Intrinsic Motivation, *Social Development, and Well-Being*. American Psychologist. Accessed at https://selfdeterminationtheory.org/SDT/documents/2000_RyanDeci_SDT.pdf.

7. Ryan, R.M. and Deci, E.L. Self-Determination Theory.

8. Ryan, R.M. and Deci, E.L. Self-Determination Theory.

9. Xiang, S., Zhang, Y., Ning, N., Wu, S., & Chen, W. (2021). How Does Leader Empowering Behavior Promote Employee Knowledge Sharing? The Perspective of Self-Determination Theory. Frontiers in Psychology. Accessed at https://www.ncbi.nlm.nih.gov/pmc/articles/PMC8439275/.

10. Zhang, X. and Bartol, K.M. (2017). Linking Empowering Leadership and Employee Creativity: The Influence of Psychological Empowerment, Intrinsic Motivation, and Creative Process Engagement. Academy of Management Journal. Accessed at https://doi.org/10.5465/amj.2010.48037118.

11. Zhang, X. Linking Empowering Leadership.

12. Zhang, X. Linking Empowering Leadership.

13. Marquet, L. David. (2016). Turn The Ship Around! A True Story Of Building Leaders By Breaking The Rules. Penguin UK.

14. Maxwell, J. C. (1993). Developing the leader within you. Nashville: T. Nelson.

15. Clutterbuck, D. (2014) Everyone Needs a Mentor. CIPD - Kogan Page.

Chapter 3

1. Lopez-Garrido, G. Self-Efficacy Theory.

2. Grover, S. and Furnham, A. (2016). Coaching as a Developmental Intervention in Organisations: A Systematic Review of Its Effectiveness and the Mechanisms Underlying It. PLoS ONE. Accessed at https://doi.org/10.1371/journal.pone.0159137.

3. Stajkovic, A. D. and Luthans, F. (1998). Self-efficacy and work-related performance: A meta-analysis. Psychological Bulletin. Accessed at https://psycnet.apa.org/record/1998-10661-005.

4. Luthans, F. and Peterson, S.J. (2003). 360-degree feedback with systematic coaching: Empirical analysis suggests a winning combination. Human Resource Management. Accessed at https://onlinelibrary.wiley.com/doi/10.1002/hrm.10083.

5. Luthans, F. and Peterson, S.J. 360-degree feedback.

6. Luthans, F. and Peterson, S.J. 360-degree feedback.

7. Luthans, F. and Peterson, S.J. 360-degree feedback.

8. Luthans, F. and Peterson, S.J. 360-degree feedback.

9. Luthans, F. and Peterson, S.J. 360-degree feedback.

10. Luthans, F. and Peterson, S.J 360-degree feedback.

11. Luthans, F. and Peterson, S.J. 360-degree feedback.

12. Ladegard, G. and Gjerde, S. (2014). Leadership coaching, leader role-efficacy, and trust in subordinates. A mixed methods study assessing leadership coaching as a leadership development tool. Leadership Quarterly. Accessed at https://www.sciencedirect.com/science/article/pii/S1048984314000058.

13. Ladegard, G. and Gjerde, S. Leadership coaching.

14. Fell, A. (2020). Job mobility in Australia. McCrindle. Accessed at https://mccrindle.com.au/uncategorized/job-mobility-in-australia/.

15. Kwan, C. (2022). Why we don't have enough workers to fill jobs (in four graphs). Australian Financial Review. Accessed at https://www.afr.com/policy/economy/why-we-don-t-have-enough-workers-to-fill-jobs-in-4-graphs-20220621-p5avcc.

16. Gallup Organization. (2022). State of the Global Workplace: 2022 Report. Accessed at https://www.gallup.com/workplace/349484/state-of-the-global-workplace.aspx.

17. Gallup. State of the Global Workplace: 2022 Report.

18. Gallup. State of the Global Workplace: 2022 Report.

19. Gallup. State of the Global Workplace: 2022 Report.

20. Gallup. State of the Global Workplace: 2022 Report.

21. Gallup. State of the Global Workplace: 2022 Report.

22. Biggs, A., Brough, P. and Barbour, J.P. (2014). Enhancing Work-Related Attitudes and Work Engagement: A Quasi-Experimental Study of the Impact of an Organizational Intervention. International Journal of Stress Management. Accessed at https://www.researchgate.net/publication/263818052_Enhancing_Work-Related_Attitudes_and_Work_Engagement_A_Quasi-Experimental_Study_of_the_Impact_of_an_Organizational_Intervention.

23. Biggs et al., (2014). Enhancing Work-Related Attitudes.

24. Biggs et al., (2014). Enhancing Work-Related Attitudes.

25. Zhang, X. (2020). The Relationship of Coaching Leadership and Innovation Behavior: Dual Mediation Model for Individuals and Teams across Levels. Open Journal of Leadership. Accessed at https://www.scirp.org/journal/paperinforcitation. aspx?paperid=98859.

26. Zhang, X. The Relationship of Coaching Leadership and Innovation.

27. Smith, C.L. (2015). How coaching helps leadership resilience: The leadership perspective. International Coaching Psychology Review. Accessed at https://organisationalpsychology.nz/wp-content/ uploads/2019/07/Volume_10_No_1_March_2015.pdf#page=8.

28. Smith, C.L. How coaching helps leadership resilience.

29. Smith, C.L. How coaching helps leadership resilience.

30. Grant, A. M., Curtayne, L. and Burton, G. (2009). Executive coaching enhances goal attainment, resilience and workplace well-being: A randomised controlled study. The Journal of Positive Psychology. Accessed at https://doi. org/10.1080/17439760902992456.

31. O'Connor, S. and Cavanagh, M. (2013). The coaching ripple effect: The effects of developmental coaching on wellbeing across organisational networks. Psychology of Well-Being Theory Research and Practice. Accessed at https://www.researchgate.net/ publication/257885642_The_coaching_ripple_effect_The_effects_ of_developmental_coaching_on_wellbeing_across_organisational_ networks.

32. O'Connor, S. and Cavanagh, M. The coaching ripple effect.

33. Grant, A. (2007). Enhancing coach skills and emotional intelligence through training. Industrial and Commercial Training. Accessed at https://www.researchgate.net/publication/235278966_Enhancing_ coach_skills_and_emotional_intelligence_through_training.

34. Smith, C.L. (2015). How coaching helps leadership resilience.

35. Murphy, M. (2016). Interruptions At Work Are Killing Your Productivity. Forbes. Accessed at https://www.forbes.com/sites/markmurphy/2016/10/30/interruptions-at-work-are-killing-your-productivity/?sh=1ee61a361689.

36. Yu, N., Collins, C., Cavanagh, M., White, K. and Fairbrother, G. (2020). Positive Coaching with Frontline Managers: Enhancing Their Effectiveness and Understanding Why. International Coaching Psychology Review. Accessed at https://onlinelibrary.wiley.com/doi/abs/10.1002/9781119656913.ch14.

37. Yuet al., (2020). Positive Coaching with Frontline Managers.

38. Nadeak, M.„ Asbari, M., Novitasari, D. and Purwanto, A. (2021). Understanding the Links between Coaching, OCB, and Individual Performance among MSME Employees. International Journal of Social and Management Studies. Accessed at https://www.researchgate.net/publication/353403166_Understanding_the_Links_between_Coaching_OCB_and_Individual_Performance_among_MSME_Employees.

39. Nadeaket al., (2021). Understanding the Links.

40. Grover, S. and Furnham, A. (2016). Coaching as a Developmental Intervention in Organisations.

41. Grover, S. and Furnham, A. (2016). Coaching as a Developmental Intervention in Organisations.

Chapter 4

1. Northouse, P.G. (2013). Leadership: Theory and Practice. Los Angeles: Sage Publications.

2. Avolio, B. J. and Bass, B. M. (1991). The Full ange Development Leadership Programs: Basic and Advanced Manuals. Binghamton, NY. Bass/Avolio & Associates.

3. Duignan, B. (2022). Dunning-Kruger effect: psychology. Encyclopedia Britannica. Accessed at https://www.britannica.com/science/Dunning-Kruger-effect.

4. Kruger, J. and Dunning, D. (1999). Unskilled and unaware of it: How difficulties in recognizing one's own incompetence lead to inflated self-assessments. Journal of Personality and Social Psychology. Accessed at https://doi.org/10.1037/0022-3514.77.6.1121.

5. Sinek, S. [@simonsinek]. (2021). [Tweet]. LinkedIn.. Retrieved 19 May 2022 from https://www.linkedin.com/posts/simonsinek_hearing-is-listening-to-what-is-said-listening-activity-6741924509055504384-Adta/.

6. Whitmore, J. (2009). Coaching For Performance: GROWing Human Potential and Purpose - The Principles and Practice of Coaching and Leadership. Nicholas Brealey.

7. Maxwell, J. (2019). What Are You Reflecting On? John C. Maxwell. Accessed at https://www.johnmaxwell.com/blog/what-are-you-reflecting-on/.

8. Liker, J.K. and Convis, G.L. (2011). The Toyota Way to Lean Leadership: Achieving and Sustaining Excellence through Leadership Development. McGraw Hill.

9. Ashdown, N. and Leow, M. (2014). Bring Out Their Best: Inspiring a Coaching Culture in Your Workplace. Palmer Higgs Books Online.

Chapter 5

1. Farrell, M. (Column Editor) (2015). Long Term Vision Creates Perspective. Journal of Library Administration. Accessed at https://www.tandfonline.com/doi/figure/10.1080/01930826.2014.995556?scroll=top&needAccess=true.

2. Farrell, M. Long Term Vision.

3. Dweck, C.S. (2007). Mindset: The New Psychology of Success. Ballantine Books.

4. Dweck, C.S. Mindset.

5. Dweck, C.S. Mindset.

6. Dweck, C.S. Mindset.

7. Moser, J.S., Schroder, H.S., Heeter, C., Moran, T.P. and Lee, Y. (2011). Mind Your Errors. Psychological Science. Accessed at https://www.researchgate.net/publication/51760065_Mind_Your_Errors.

8. Moser et al., (2011). Mind Your Errors.

9. Moser et al., (2011). Mind Your Errors.

10. HBR Editors. (2014).. How Companies Can Profit from a 'Growth Mindset. Harvard Business Review. Accessed at https://hbr.org/2014/11/how-companies-can-profit-from-a-growth-mindset.

11. Bennis, W. and Nanus, B. (1986). Leaders: Strategies for taking Charge. Harper & Row.

12. Rahman, M.M. and Akhter, B. (2021). The impact of investment in human capital on bank performance: evidence from Bangladesh. Future Business Journal. Accessed at https://fbj.springeropen.com/articles/10.1186/s43093-021-00105-5.

13. Greenleaf, R. (2020). Perfect is not perfect. Greenleaf.org. Accessed at https://www.greenleaf.org/perfect-not-perfect/.

14. Livingston, J. S. (2003). Pygmalion in Management. Harvard Business Review. Accessed at https://hbr.org/2003/01/pygmalion-in-management.

15. Livingston. Pygmalion in Management.

16. Rosenthal, R. and Jacobson, L. (2003). Pygmalion in the Classroom: Teacher Expectation and Pupils' Intellectual Development. Crown House Publishing.

17. Rosenthal and Jacobsen. Pygmalion in the Classroom.

18. Kierein, N.M. and Gold, M.A. (2000). Pygmalion in work organizations: a meta-analysis. Journal of Organizational Behavior. Accessed at https://www.jstor.org/stable/3100361.

19. Kierein and Gold. Pygmalion in work organizations.

20. Turkmenoglu, M.A. (2019). Investigating Benefits and Drawbacks of Employee Empowerment in the Sector of Hospitality. International Research Journal of Business Studies. Accessed at https://www.researchgate.net/publication/332198747_Investigating_Benefits_and_Drawbacks_of_Employee_Empowerment_in_the_Sector_of_Hospitality

21. Folkman, J. and Zenger, J. (2009). The Extraordinary Leader: Turning Good Managers into Great Leaders. McGraw Hill.

Chapter 6

1.   Haney, W. V. (1979). Communication and interpersonal relations. Homewood, IL. Irwin.

2.   Husman, R. C., Lahiff, J. M., & Penrose, J. M. (1988). Business communication: Strategies and skills. Chicago. Dryden Press.

3.   LinkedIn Pressroom. (2020). New research shows how leaders should be preparing for the future of work. Accessed at https://news.linkedin.com/2020/january/future-of-leadership.

4.   Rogers, C. (1995). A Way of Being. Mariner Books

5.   DeAngelis, T. (2019). Better relationships with patients lead to better outcomes: A good relationship is essential to helping the client connect with, remain in and get the most from therapy. American Psychological Association. Accessed at https://www.apa.org/monitor/2019/11/ce-corner-relationships.

6.   Sinek, S. [@simonsinek]. (2013). [Tweet]. Twitter. Accessed at https://twitter.com/simonsinek/status/324907002490925056?lang=en

7.   Mehrabian, A. and Ferris, S. R. (1967). Inference of attitudes from nonverbal communication in two channels. Journal of Consulting Psychology. Accessed at https://psycnet.apa.org/doiLanding?doi=10.1037%2Fh0024648.

8. Mehrabian, A. Inference of attitudes from nonverbal communication.

9. Leathers, D. and Eaves, M. (2015.) Successful Nonverbal Communication: Principles and Applications. Routledge.

10. The Public Health Quality Improvement Handbook. Five Whys and Five Hows.. ASQ Quality Press. Accessed at https://asq.org/quality-resources/five-whys.

11. Toyota. (n.d.). Toyota Production System.Accessed at https://global.toyota/en/company/vision-and-philosophy/production-system/.

12. Liker, J. K. (2004). The Toyota way: 14 management principles from the world's greatest manufacturer. McGraw-Hill.

13. Covey, S. (2004). The 7 Habits of Highly Effective People: Powerful Lessons in Personal Change. Free Press.

14. Cherry, K. (2020). What Is the Negativity Bias? Verywell Mind. Accessed at https://www.verywellmind.com/negative-bias-4589618#.

15. Koudenburg, N. (2011). Disrupting the flow: How brief silences in group conversations affect social needs. Journal of Experimental Social Psychology. Accessed at https://www.rug.nl/staff/n.koudenburg/koudenburgetal.2011.pdf.

16. Koudenburg, N. Disrupting the flow.

17. Koudenburg, N. Disrupting the flow.

18. Taylor, C. (2015). Walking the Talk: Building a Culture for Success. Cornerstone.

19. Kiyosaki, R. (2017). Rich Dad Poor Dad: What the Rich Teach Their Kids About Money That the Poor and Middle Class Do Not! Plata Publishing.

20. Hall, K. (2012). Understanding Validation: A Way to Communicate Acceptance. Psychology Today. Accessed at https://www.psychologytoday.com/us/blog/pieces-mind/201204/understanding-validation-way-communicate-acceptance.

Chapter 7

1. Doran, G. T. (1981). There's a S.M.A.R.T. Way to Write Management's Goals and Objectives. Management Review. Accessed at https://community.mis.temple.edu/mis0855002fall2015/files/2015/10/S.M.A.R.T-Way-Management-Review.pdf.

2. Hill, N. (1937). Think and Grow Rich. G&D Media.

3. Meares, A. (2009). The Anna Meares Story. New Holland Publishers.

4. Meares, A. The Anna Meares Story.

5. Meares, A. The Anna Meares Story.

6. Berkman E.T. (2018). The Neuroscience of Goals and Behavior Change. Consulting Psychology Journal. Accessed at https://www.ncbi.nlm.nih.gov/pmc/articles/PMC5854216/.

7. Matthews, G. (2007). The Impact of Commitment, Accountability, and Written Goals on Goal *Achievement*. Dominican Scholar. Accessed at https://scholar.dominican.edu/psychology-faculty-conference-presentations/3.

8. Matthew, G. The Impact of Commitment.

9. Riezler, K. (1944). The Social Psychology of Fear. American Journal of Sociology. Accessed at https://www.jstor.org/stable/2771546.

10. Miller, G.A. (1956). The magical number seven, plus or minus two: Some limits on our capacity for processing information. Psychological Review. Accessed at https://doi.org/10.1037/h0043158.

Chapter 8

1. Whitmore. Coaching for Performance.

2. Papathanasiou I.V, Kleisiaris, C.F.,, Fradelos, E.C., Kakou, K., and Kourkouta L. (2014). Critical Thinking: The Development of an Essential Skill for Nursing Students. Acta Informatica Medica. Accessed at https://www.ncbi.nlm.nih.gov/pmc/articles/PMC4216424/.

3. Papathanasiou et.al., (2014). Critical Thinking.

Chapter 9

1. Clardy, A. (2018). 70-20-10 and the Dominance of Informal Learning: A Fact in Search of Evidence. Human Resource Development Review. Accessed at https://journals.sagepub.com/doi/abs/10.1177/1534484318759399?journalCode=hrda.

2. Clardy, A. 70-20-10.

3. Depree, M. (1989). Leadership Is an Art. Currency.

4. Professional Standards Councils.(n.d.). What is a profession? Accessed at https://www.psc.gov.au/what-is-a-profession.

5. Lee, M., Idris, M., and Tuckey, M. (2019). Supervisory coaching and performance feedback as mediators of the relationships between leadership styles, work engagement, and turnover intention. Human Resource Development International. Accessed at https://psycnet.apa.org/record/2019-24493-004.

6. Peterson, S.J. and Luthans, F. (2003). The positive impact and development of hopeful leaders. Leadership & Organization Development Journal. Accessed at https://psycnet.apa.org/record/2009-18905-003.

7. Peterson, S.J. and Luthans, F. The positive impact and development of hopeful leaders.

8. Peterson, S.J. and Luthans, F. The positive impact and development of hopeful leaders.

9. Peterson, S.J. and Luthans, F. The positive impact and development of hopeful leaders.

10. Price, M. and Williams, T. (2015). When Doing Wrong Feels So Right: Normalization of Deviance. Journal of Patient Safety. Accessed at https://journals.lww.com/journalpatientsafety/Abstract/2018/03000/When_Doing_Wrong_Feels_So_Right__Normalization_of.1.aspx.

11. To, W. and Yu, B.T.W. (2022). Effects of Difficult Coworkers on Employees' Responses in Macao's Public Organizations—The Mediating Role of Perceived Stress. Administrative Sciences. Accessed at https://www.mdpi.com/2076-3387/12/1/6/pdf?version=1640700263.

12. Clear, J. (2022). 3-2-1: Prioritization, making the most of what you have, and reading as a form of travel. James Clear. Accessed at https://jamesclear.com/3-2-1/may-12-2022.

Chapter 10

1. Baldoni, J. (2009). Lead Your Boss: The Subtle Art of Managing Up Hardcover. AMACOM.

2. Khoshhal, K.I. and Guraya, S.Y. (2016). Leaders produce leaders and managers produce followers. A systematic review of the desired competencies and standard settings for physicians' leadership. Saudi Medical Journal. Accessed at https://doi.org/10.15537/smj.2016.10.15620.

3. Rogacka, O. (2020). 12 Stories From Leaders: Their Mistakes and Lessons Learned. Success by Live Chat. Accessed at https://www.livechat.com/success/stories-from-leaders-mistakes-lessons-learned/.

Chapter 11

1. Maxwell, J.(2019). What Are You Reflecting On? John C. Maxwell. Accessed at https://www.johnmaxwell.com/blog/what-are-you-reflecting-on/

2. DiMenichi, B.C., Ceceli, A.O., Bhanji, J.P., and Tricomi, E. (2019). Effects of Expressive Writing on Neural Processing During Learning. Frontiers. Accessed at https://www.frontiersin.org/articles/10.3389/fnhum.2019.00389/full.

3. Clear, J. (2021). 3-2-1: How to get motivated and learn faster, and the power of attention. James Clear. Accessed at https://jamesclear.com/3-2-1/june-17-2021.

4. The Bridge. (n.d.). Strategies for Life-Work Balance. Accessed at https://www.acc.af.mil/Portals/92/Strategies%20for%20Life-Work%20Balance.pdf

5. Chau, S. and Cheung, C. (2017). 'Bringing Life to Learning': A Study of Active Learning in Hospitality Education. The Asia-Pacific Education Researcher. Accessed at https://link.springer.com/article/10.1007/s40299-017-0333-6.

6. Maxwell, J. (2012). The 15 Invaluable Laws of Growth: Live Them and Reach Your Potential. Center Street.

7. Bungay Stanier, M. (2016). The Coaching Habit: Say Less, Ask More & Change the Way You Lead Forever. Box of Crayons Press.

8. Folkman, J.R. and Zegman, J.H. (2019). The Extraordinary Leader: Turning Good Managers into Great Leaders. McGraw Hill

9. Joubert, J. (1899). Joubert: A Selection From His Thoughts. Katharine Lyttelton, trans. Dodd, Mead & Co. Accessed at www.bartleby.com/354/.

Chapter 12

1. Crane, T. (2012). The Heart of Coaching: Using Transformational Coaching to Create a High-Performance Coaching Culture. FTA Press.

2. David, S. (2016). Emotional Agility. Avery Publishing Group.

3. Royal Australian Air Force. Air Force Strategy 2017–2027. Accessed at https://raafsca.files.wordpress.com/2012/10/air-force-strategy-2017-2027.pdf.

4. Australian Government Department of Defence. Air Force Strategy Key Highlights. Accessed at https://www.airforce.gov.au/sites/default/files/air_force_strategy.pdf.

5. Ashdown, N. Bring Out Their Best.

6. Ashdown, N. Bring Out Their Best.

Chapter 13

1. Maxwell, J. (2009). Self-Improvement 101: What Every Leader Needs to Know. HarperCollins Leadership.

2. Sonnentag, S., Cheng, B.H. and Parker, S.L. (2022). Recovery from work: Advancing the field toward the future. Annual Review of Organizational Psychology and Organizational Behaviour. Accessed at https://psycnet.apa.org/record/2022-34328-002.

www.ingramcontent.com/pod-product-compliance
Lightning Source LLC
Chambersburg PA
CBHW071336210326
41597CB00015B/1469